Field Officer Resource Guide

American Correctional Association

Acknowledgments

ACA would like to thank the authors of this book who gave freely of their time and efforts to share their expertise with others in their field. Special thanks go to Anthony Walsh, Ph.d., Department of Criminal Justice Administration at Boise State University, who reviewed early drafts of the books; James E. Dare, director of the Adult Probation Department in Montgomery County, Ohio, who not only reviewed the book, but also supplied information on ACA standards that apply to each chapter and some of the photos that appear in this book; and Marsha Bailey, communications coordinator for the Georgia State Board of Pardons and Paroles, for contributing many of the photos used in this book.

Perry M. Johnson, *President*
James A. Gondles, Jr., *Executive Director*
Karen L. Kushner, *Director of Communications and Publications*
Marianna Nunan, *Managing Editor*
Jennifer A. Nichols, *Production Editor*
Ann M. Tontodonato, *Cover Designer*

Photo Credits
Photos on pages 17, 26, 33, 43, 44, 46, 58, 63, 65, 77, 83, 91, and 95 are courtesy of Marsha Bailey, communications coordinator for the Georgia State Board of Pardons and Paroles. Photos on pages 14, 36, 50, 51, 53, and 71 are courtesy of James E. Dare, director of the Adult Probation Department in Montgomery County, Ohio.

Printed in the United States of America by United Book Press, Inc., Baltimore, Md.

ISBN 1-56991-001-4

Contents

Foreword iv

1. History of Probation and Parole 1

2. Presentence Investigation Reports 12

3. Assessment and Supervision Planning 19

4. Supervision of Probationers 31

5. Supervision of Parolees 41

6. Intermediate Sanctions and Probation 48

7. Electronic Monitoring 57

8. Drug Testing in Probation and Parole Supervision 62

9. Special Needs Offenders on Probation and Parole 68

10. Probation and Parole and the Community 82

11. Victims 88

12. Managing Change in Probation and Parole 99

Foreword

Community corrections is beginning to feel the burden of society's crowded prisons and jails, with more offenders being routed into supervised community corrections programs. This, and considerable financial constraints, has put extraordinary demands on probation and parole agencies and on the staff who supervise offenders on probation and parole.

The job of a field officer is demanding and requires skill in several different areas, including interpersonal communication, report writing, planning, resource management, and supervision. Many field officers supplement the knowledge and skills they acquired in school and formal training programs with skills acquired on the job.

Field Officer Resource Guide is written for the beginning field officer and the criminal justice student. Each chapter is written by experts in probation and parole. These professionals share the expertise they have gained in the classroom and through years of working in the field. The chapters cover topics that are important and helpful to those in community corrections. Some of the topics covered are preparing presentence investigation reports, assessment and supervision planning, supervising probationers and parolees, using intermediate sanctions, using drug testing, working with special needs offenders, and interacting with victims.

When used as a training guide, either in self-study or as part of an agency's formal training program, it will help field officers to embrace, understand, and carry out the two-fold mission of community corrections—to supervise the offender in the community and to protect the public's safety and interests.

James A. Gondles, Jr.
ACA Executive Director

1

History of Probation and Parole

By Alvin W. Cohn

Over the centuries, society's beliefs about the nature of people changed from the eighteenth century Classical point of view (where a person was seen as governed by free will and pleasure and pain principles) to the twentieth century Positive tradition (where a person was viewed as being governed by forces beyond his or her will). Each of these beliefs resulted in ways to control crime and delinquency as well as to punish offenders.

During the Classical period, society sought to exercise control through the law and with fixed kinds of punishments that were meant to serve as deterrents. The individual's *crime* was the focus. Positivists, on the other hand, sought to control lawbreakers by examining them as individuals and by examining those forces that were thought to influence their deviant behavior. During the Positivist period the *individual* was scrutinized, rather than the crime itself.

The Positive view gave rise to probation and parole, both of which permit offenders to remain in the community after being convicted of an offense. Although programs and services rendered by probation and parole officers may seem similar, there are significant differences between these two punishments, especially in terms of the offender's legal status and the source of placement into this status.

An offender on probation has been convicted of a crime and is sentenced to a term of probation by the sentencing judge. An offender placed on parole has been convicted of a crime, sentenced to a term in a correctional facility (prison or jail), but released from that facility by a paroling authority (usually a parole board) prior to the expiration of the sentence.

Probationers and parolees, who may have committed misdemeanors or felonies and who may be adults or juveniles, are placed under the supervision of a probation or parole officer. The officer is responsible for monitoring the offender's behavior, ensuring that any special terms and conditions of community supervision are followed, and ensuring public safety. Offenders are required to report to the officer on a regular basis and follow the conditions imposed on them.

Probationers who violate imposed conditions appear before a judge, who has the authority to revoke probation and institute a period of incarceration. Parolees who violate imposed conditions appear before a parole board. The parole board has the authority to revoke the parolee's freedom and return him or her to prison (or jail) to complete the original sentence.

Probation is administered by city, county, state, or federal agencies throughout the country, while adult and juvenile parole services, for the most part, are administered by state agencies or the federal government. In some jurisdictions, misdemeanant parole is administered by a county-based parole agency. Canada uses the same structural approach to probation and parole, with

Dr. Alvin Cohn *is the founder and president of Administration of Justice Services, Inc., which is based in Rockville, Maryland.*

responsibility shared by federal, provincial, and territorial governments.

Probation

Early History

The concept of probation developed from earlier practices several hundred years ago in England and the United States. These practices were intended to lessen or otherwise mitigate the severities of the penal code. It is commonly believed that the concept of probation originated from English Common Law, where the courts as early as the fourteenth century were presumed to have the power to *suspend* sentences for specified purposes and periods. Although it is unclear exactly which precedents permitted the process of what is now referred to as probation, there is some agreement that benefit of clergy, judicial reprieve, recognizance, bail, and filing of cases all made some contribution (Grinnell 1941; United Nations 1951; Cohn 1976).

In the United States, the development of what is known today as probation is often traced to the work of John Augustus in Boston in 1841. In fact, it is believed that Augustus was the first to use the term "probation." Dressler (1959), writing from a historical point of view, asserts:

> The social climate was right for the birth of probation in the nineteenth century (and in the United States). Thoughtful observers had become convinced that prisons were not "teaching a lesson," penitentiaries were not making inmates penitent. It was also becoming clear that suspension of sentence without provision for supervision and guidance of the released person served little purpose. So it was that Matthew Davenport Hill, of Birmingham, England, pioneered in his country in 1841, the very year that John Augustus performed a like service in Boston for the United States.

In the early years, those who provided probation services (almost exclusively to adult offenders) were volunteers who developed a basic program model, including such activities as investigations, reports, home visits, and job placements. However, early probation began not with a desire to rehabilitate the offender, but as a reflection of a simple humanitarian wish to keep less serious or first offenders from undergoing the corrupting influences of incarceration (England 1957).

The first statutory provision for probation, which included language that authorized the hiring and payment of probation officers, occurred in Massachusetts in 1878. According to the statute, the mayor of Boston was authorized to appoint and pay a probation officer and authorized the municipal court to place offenders on probation. The legislature extended this power to all other mayors in the state in 1880, and in 1891 it "...made mandatory the appointment of probation officers by lower court judges" (Sutherland & Cressey 1970). The first state commission on probation was established in Massachusetts in 1908 (Tappan 1960).

Missouri enacted the next law in 1897. By 1900, Illinois, Minnesota, New Jersey, Rhode Island, and Vermont had passed probation legislation. There were many variations in the early statutes: Illinois and Minnesota provided for juvenile probation only, and Rhode Island excluded certain categories of offenders from probation consideration. Vermont used only the county plan of organization instead of statewide services, while Rhode Island had a statewide program and state-controlled administration.

These probation services, for the most part, were for adult offenders only. It was not until the creation of the first juvenile court in Chicago in 1899 that juvenile probation gained a foothold. By 1945, all states had passed legislation authorizing juvenile probation, but it was not until 1957 that provision for adult probation services had been legislated by all of the states (Dressler 1959).

In a report prepared in 1967, the National Council on Crime and Delinquency stated:

> Development of the legal basis for probation was accompanied by a definition of duties and responsibilities of the probation officer, formulation of criteria for granting probation, provision for and definition of the presentence investigation, authorization of the imposition of probation conditions, and revocation, and refinement of policies, practices, and forms of administrative structure.

The early services of the unsalaried probation officers were generally viewed as adequate because not much was expected of them in terms of programs. However, with the application of psychoanalytic theories and the increasing activities of social welfare enthusiasts in the areas of crime and delinquency control, the growth of professionalized probation services, with trained officers, was inevitable (Cohn 1976).

In *Social Diagnosis* (1917), the founder of modern social work, Mary Richmond, discussed the emerging role of the probation officer and the processes by which the officer was supposed to gather critical information about offenders. Richmond pointed out the now obvious relationship between social casework and probation services and suggested that differences in settings do indeed bear on practice. She stated: "...a probation officer is known to come from the court and to represent it, certain conditions, favorable and the reverse, are created by this fact; the officer has more authority but less freedom than a social worker who lacks the court background."

Since 1898, when the Summer School of Philanthropic Workers was established in New York, social casework has been identified with probation (and parole) services, especially as the ideal model by which change could be brought about within the offenders being served. Although less favored today because agencies have difficulty recruiting trained caseworkers and because of high caseloads, casework, remains the standard by which probation services are rendered.

Social casework as both a model and a standard may have declined in recent years, not only as a result of the reasons cited, but as a consequence of a shift in public policy in corrections from that of rehabilitation of the offender to one of social control. Yet where casework remains a viable model, the provision of professional and high-level services in such an authoritarian setting as a court remains a significantly unresolved dilemma for practicing probation officers. Notwithstanding this, many probation agencies stipulate that a master's degree in social work is the *preferred* qualification for those seeking employment.

Use of Probation

As probation services increased throughout the United States, various legislatures frequently provided restrictions or exclusions as to who was eligible for such a sentence. With the advent of stricter controls and guidelines on sentencing (reducing judicial discretion), more and more legislatures have imposed exclusions. For the most part, probation controls have been provided for in only the most serious of offenses, especially where life sentences or capital punishment has been provided or where the offender is legally described as "chronic."

The American Bar Association has taken issue with these restrictions, and in fact, its Standards Relating to the Administration of Criminal Justice (1974) states:

> The legislature should authorize the sentencing court in every case to impose a sentence of probation. Exceptions to this principle are not favored and, if made, should be limited to the most serious offenses.

The report goes on to list five reasons why probation should be the desirable disposition in appropriate cases:

(i)   it maximizes the liberty of the individual while at the same time vindicating the authority of the law and effectively protecting the public from further violations of the law;

(ii) it affirmatively promotes the rehabilitation of the offender by continuing normal community contacts;

(iii) it avoids the negative and frequently stultifying effects of confinement which often severely and unnecessarily complicate the reintegration of the offender into the community;

(iv) it greatly reduces the financial cost to the public treasury of an effective correctional system;

(v)   it minimizes the impact of the conviction upon innocent dependents of the offender.

As significant as the relative yet increasing use of probation might be in both the United States and Canada, the disparity in its use also is significant. Legislation always authorizes but does not mandate the use of probation as a sentence. That is, even where sentencing guidelines are in effect—depending on the nature of the case, the personal belief systems of judges, availability of community resources, and other factors—judges may use probation as an alternative to other sentences if they wish, but are not generally obligated to do so.

One of the primary duties of a probation officer is that of investigating the background of a sentenced offender to provide the judge with relevant and pertinent information about the offender. This information helps to guide the judge in his or her rational sentencing decision. Judges tend to follow the recommendations contained in the presentence investigation reports, whether these recommendations are for probation or for incarceration. This suggests that the final disposition of an offender in court is more in the hands of probation officers than in the hands of the judges who actually pronounce the sentences (Cohn 1970; Lohman, Whal & Carter 1965–67; Robison 1969; Cohn & Ferriter 1990).

Research suggests that judges follow probation officer recommendations in as many as 90 to 95 percent of the cases. Thus, probation, which used to be tolerated by many judges and used as an exception in sentencing, now has become an indispensable tool in sentencing in most courts in both the United States and Canada.

Probation Structures

Probation is provided for adults and juveniles, misdemeanants and felons. Moreover, probation agencies are administered either by judges (judiciary) or by administrators within some kind of department housed in the executive branch of government. Historically, because probation developed as a service of the courts, and in fact as a form of sentence, much of its control and administration rests within a court structure. This is especially true for juveniles.

As a consequence of its judicial roots, it is not uncommon to find that most probation officers, according to statute, must be appointed by the court and, particularly, by the (presiding) judge. In the U.S. federal system, for example, probation officers are appointed by the various federal judges, but technically only on the recommendation and approval of the Administrative Office of the U.S. Courts—the administrative arm of the federal judiciary. The same holds at the state level, where, for example, in Massachusetts the Office of the Commissioner of Probation must technically approve the appointments made by judges of the various courts throughout the commonwealth.

Probation developed as a service of the courts, and much of its control and administration rests within a judicial structure.

Sutherland and Cressey (1970) commented on this practice:

> The stated objections [to the judge administering probation services]...are First, the work of supervision is essentially administrative, not judicial.... Second, the judge is not able to handle the administrative work efficiently.... Consequently, there has been a trend toward the other method of appointment and supervision of probation officers.

This other method is that of probation services being housed within the executive branch of government. Although this is generally uncommon at the county level of government, it is usually found where statewide services are provided. Here, probation is located either within a department of corrections or in an independent agency. At the juvenile level, where probation is generally a function of the juvenile court, agency-wise it is usually within the judiciary. An exception can be found in Maryland, where services are statewide and a part of the executive branch of government.

Historically, one of the reasons for moving probation from the judiciary to the executive branch has been to upgrade the quality and credentials of probation officers. When the judges appointed officers, it was not uncommon in the past for such appointments to be primarily political. That is, service to the right political party became more of a qualifying credential for appointment than experience or education. This has changed dramatically over the years; however, vestiges of patronage, especially at the county level, remain the hallmark for appointments.

Where probation officers are employed by county or state departments of personnel, credentials for appointment usually are higher, and most of these employees in the executive branch of government tend to have civil service status.

Whether probation is part of the judiciary or the executive branch of government does not reduce the obligation of the probation agency or its staff to serve the courts and its judges. Although the role of the agency and the officer is to provide services to offenders, both have a primary duty to ensure the demands of the court are fulfilled, especially when it comes to the supervision process (following probation conditions) and the investigatory process (completing presentence investigations). Thus, no matter where the agency is located, the courts are to be served and the requirements of the judges met.

Recently, private probation agencies—nongovernmental organizations working under contract with either the court or the political jurisdiction to provide probation services to offenders—have been created. These private organizations serve courts handling misdemeanants, but this may change in the future. The movement for privatized services, whether a trend or not, has come about primarily to fill a void in actual services. This void has occurred as a consequence of existing probation agencies being overworked and overloaded or where probation services simply have not been available to certain categories of offenders—particularly misdemeanants. Private probation services can be found in Arizona, Florida, Kentucky, and Utah.

Regardless of the nature, scope, structure, and auspices of probation services, only the following three variables remain constant irrespective of organizational structure or geographical location of the probation agency (Cohn 1976):

1. Every agency operates according to statutory authority.

2. Every agency serves clients who are sentenced to probation by judicial action.

3. Every chief administrative officer of a probation agency is answerable to some other superior, including judges, chief administrators, commissioners or directors of large agencies, or elected state or local officials.

Approximately forty years ago, Turnbladth (1956) summarized the nature and importance of probation as follows:

> I suggest that we think of the probation service not as a resource which the legislatures are being en-

couraged to expand as one of the many important public services. Rather, we have to think of the right of the court to probation service, and the *responsibility* of the legislature to guarantee its adequacy in the courts…. Probation service—the keystone of the sentencing structure—is…an integral part of the court and the judicial process. The courts have a right to this service, a right no less substantial than their right to equipment and staff required for adjudication of guilt or innocence….

Parole

The classic and most accepted definition of parole is that provided in the U.S. Attorney General's Survey of Release Procedures (1939): "…release of an offender from a penal or correctional institution, after he has served a portion of his sentence, under the continued custody of the state and under conditions that permit his reincarceration in the event of misbehavior." Thus, for an offender to be placed on parole, he or she must first serve a period of time in a correctional facility as a result of a sentence imposed by a judge. Probation differs from parole in that the offender is sentenced to a term of probation without first having to spend time in a jail or prison.

Although some jurisdictions impose limitations on the use of parole and some, in fact, have abolished parole, offenders generally can be paroled in the United States and Canada.

Parole developed almost simultaneously with probation, especially in the United States, and primarily as a result of the Positive movement. As psychological theories about why people behave as they do gained popularity, public officials attempted to control crime and delinquency through greater understanding of the individual. It was hoped that through such understanding and individualization of the offender, it would be possible to control misbehavior through treatment and rehabilitation efforts. It was this "rehabilitative ideal" (Allen 1964) that helped to create parole, and probation services.

Early History of Parole

The foundation for what is called parole today was introduced in some of the European penal codes of the sixteenth and seventeenth centuries. Commutation, for example, was first used as a sort of pardon. Later it was used as an incentive for good behavior in prison, enabling the inmate to earn an unconditional discharge before the expiration of a sentence. This is the origin of the "good time" concept, a device that was used in the Amsterdam

Tuchthuys between 1599 and 1603, with juvenile offenders in France in 1832, and adopted in the 1805 Cadiz Code in Spain and in a general code in 1807 (Giardini 1959).

The indeterminate sentence, whereby offenders can be detained for as long as the authorities wish (without any fixed or determinate sentence), serves as the foundation of parole. It goes as far back as the Middle Ages, where it was conceived as a means of securing social protection against habitual offenders. It was first introduced in the Code of 1532 under Charles V of Germany and again in the Code of 1768 of Maria Theresa. It appeared in similar form in the Colonial Law of Connecticut in 1769 (Giardini 1959).

It is commonly thought that parole in the United States was developed in the 1840s as a direct result of European and Australian measures of ticket-of-leave and license. However, the former chairman of the New York State Board of Parole claims this is a misconception (Moran 1945):

> Parole did not develop from any specific source of experiment, but is an outgrowth of a number of independent measures, including the conditional pardon, apprenticeship by indenture, the transportation of criminals to America and Australia, the English and Irish experiences with the system of ticket-of-leave, and the work of American prison reformers during the nineteenth century.

According to Rubin (1973), some elements of contemporary parole as a method of conditional release are found in the model developed by Captain Alexander Maconochie in 1840, who was then head of England's penal colony at Norfolk Island. This was a system that was devised after the transportation system (sending convicted offenders off to other countries—especially colonies) proved to be a failure:

> Maconochie found that a man under a time sentence thinks only how he is to cheat that time, and while it away; he evades labor, because he has no interest in it whatever, and he has no desires to please the officers under whom he is placed, because they cannot serve him essentially; they cannot in any way promote his liberation.

Maconochie developed a system whereby inmates would be awarded marks for industry, labor, and good conduct that could be used to earn their way out of confinement. The number of marks required for such release depended, in part, on the original offense for which the offender had been convicted and was balanced by the loss of marks whenever the inmate misbehaved.

The U.S. Attorney General's survey (1939) adds that a second feature of the Maconochie system was the series of four stages leading to freedom. The first stage was absolute confinement and adherence to rigid disciplinary rules. The second was participation in government chain gangs. The third was limited liberty within a confined area. The fourth was a grant of ticket-of-leave for conditional freedom, followed finally by absolute freedom.

Despite Maconochie's optimism about the system of marks and progressive stages of freedom, the plan was neither widely followed, even at Norfolk, nor subsequently adopted in England to any great extent. Its principal flaw was the lack of supervision over the released inmates, which apparently was remedied to some extent first by Sir Joshua Webb in 1846 and then by Sir Walter Crofton, who in 1854 became director of the Irish prison system.

Crofton followed a plan of progressive stages of liberty for inmates, and on being granted a ticket-of-leave, the inmate was also given a list of specific and rather restrictive conditions of liberty. If any of the conditions were violated, the authorities would be able to revoke the liberty. In addition to being subject to reincarceration, the liberated offender also had to make periodic reports to police officials (Rubin 1973).

Crofton apparently made full use of the Penal Servitude Act, which provided three stages of penal treatment. The last of these was the ticket-of-leave, which was granted on the basis of visible evidence that the offender had been reformed in prison. The act also provided for revocation of license if the inmate did not follow prescribed conditions of release, which resulted in return to prison (Giardini 1959).

Notwithstanding these progressive efforts to arrange for the conditional release of inmates, there remained the basic weakness of the absence of supervision of the inmate in the community—a weakness that apparently was recognized in the Australian experiment. This flaw was brought to the attention of the public as a result of an outbreak of serious crimes shortly after the ticket-of-leave became widely used. As a consequence, the police were assisted in this process of supervision by inmates' aid societies, which were partly subsidized by the government (Cohn 1976).

Parole in the United States

The development of parole in the United States cannot be understood without also understanding the development of inmates' aid societies and the indeterminate sentence.

Giardini (1959) comments on the indeterminate sentence and its relationship to parole:

> The indeterminate sentence idea became quite widespread in Europe and especially in Germany, but disappeared in the middle of the 19th century. Montesinos in Spain...in 1835 and Obermaier in Germany between 1830 and 1862 not only made use of the indeterminate sentence, but also introduced vocational trades.... Under (Obermaier's)...regime, release from prison was determined largely by evidence of reformation. He also introduced supervision after release by agencies other than the police. In 1837 he suggested the organization of prisoners' aid societies (which)...were sponsored by the government and were composed of volunteer workers who supervised and cared for released prisoners.

This process of volunteer supervision, incidentally, is similar to that which was originally developed when probation was initiated in the United States.

Although churches had a long history in dealing with those who were "afflicted," sick, or in prison, the first secular organization in the United States to help people in prison was formed in 1776. It was known as the Philadelphia Society for Assisting Distressed Prisoners. Its purpose was to collect and distribute food and clothes to inmates in the local jail. The American Revolution interrupted its program, so it disbanded after only nineteen months of work. However, it was reorganized in 1787 under the name the Philadelphia Society for Alleviating the Miseries of the Public Prisons—later known as the Philadelphia Prison Society.

The work of the group spread and provided impetus for the development of similar groups throughout the Northeast, including the Boston Prison Discipline Society, the New Jersey Howard Society, the Prisoners' Friend Association of Boston, and the Prison Association of New York. These organizations were active in prison reform and the amelioration of criminal procedures in general.

Their growth also coincided with changes in penal laws and practices as professionalism, economic growth, and concern for the individual progressed. In 1870, representatives of many of these groups met in Cincinnati under the name of the American Prison Association (now the American Correctional Association) and adopted a set of Principles, which were reaffirmed in 1970 at the centennial meeting of ACA.

One of the Principles was that of shortening the term of imprisonment as a reward for good conduct. In fact, it had first been legally recognized in the New York "good time" law of 1817. The indeterminate sentence itself was first introduced with the establishment of the Houses of Refuge for children in New York City in 1825. "This furnished another pattern of shortening the time served in the institution on the basis of good conduct...," which was the same motivational force used in Europe with adult offenders (Giardini 1959). Spurred by the 1870 American Prison Association meeting, the concept was introduced in every political jurisdiction in the United States, with the last law passed in Maryland in 1916.

It was the indeterminate sentence that gave authority to "professionals" to decide what to do to an offender and for what length of time. Thus, even though a judge could sentence an offender to twenty years of incarceration, the parole board, by law, had the authority to make the final decision on how long the offender would actually remain incarcerated before release. The board, therefore, could release him or her to parole at any time (with some restrictions) before the twenty years was up.

These early forms of conditional release set a pattern that is still followed in most jurisdictions in the United States and Canada today. Inmates who abide by institution rules are rewarded by legislated authority with a reduction in their sentence.

As a result of successful experiences in these release endeavors, another pattern developed that demanded that inmates agree to a contract with the releasing authority regarding postrelease behavior. Today, this is generally called a "parole agreement," and almost all jurisdictions require the parolee to sign such a document. Among the conditions to which the released inmate had to agree (and which is still practiced today) was the recognition that if the terms and conditions for release were violated or abridged in any way, the parolee would be returned to the institution to finish the original sentence. In the language of today, this would occur as a result of a "technical violation" as opposed to the consequence of committing a new offense. (A return to prison to complete an original sentence as a result of a technical violation is the consequence of an administrative decision by the paroling authority; the sentence that results from a conviction for a new offense is a decision made by a judge.)

Almost without exception, to assist former inmates in adjusting to their return to society from prison and to avoid being reincarcerated, most of the early releasing authorities required some form of community-based supervision, usually by volunteers. Children who had been released from the houses of refuge tended to be supervised by their "masters" because they tended in effect to be indentured. Adults were generally not indentured but were supervised by members of a prison society.

As early as 1822, the Philadelphia Society for Alleviating the Miseries of Public Prisons recognized the importance of caring for discharged inmates, but it was not until 1851 that the society appointed two agents to supervise men who had been released from the Philadelphia County Prison and the Penitentiary. It was at this time, too, that the use of the word "parole" replaced "conditional liberation" as the process for shortening imprisonment.

S. G. Howe of Boston is alleged to have been the first person to use this term when he wrote a letter to the Prison Association of New York in 1846 (Killinger 1951):

> I believe there are many prisoners who might be so trained as to be left upon their parole during the last period of their imprisonment with safety.

Massachusetts was the first state to arrange for a salaried employee to supervise parolees. In 1845, the state appointed an agent to help released inmates obtain employment, tools, clothing, and transportation with the aid of public funds. However, the experiment in Massachusetts did not catch on, and it was many years before releasing authorities were able to depend on public employees to supervise and otherwise manage those released early from prisons.

The first indeterminate sentence law was passed in Michigan in 1869 at the instigation of Zebulon R. Brockway, a well-known penologist. Although the law was declared unconstitutional, Brockway, as superintendent at Elmira Reformatory, was successful in 1876 in having a similar law passed in New York that was upheld as constitutional. Thus, a complete correctional process was established for the first time.

> [The law]...comprised not only the use of the indeterminate sentence, but also a system of grading the inmates, compulsory education, and a careful system of selection for parole. Supervision of the released prisoners was provided by volunteer citizens who were known as guardians. One of the conditions of parole was that the parolee must report to the guardian on the first of each month. Later, written reports were required and submitted to the institution after they had been countersigned by the employer and the guardian (Giardini 1959).

The basic principles of parole, as spelled out in the first law, have been carried through the years and serve as the basis of much of contemporary parole philosophy in the United States and Canada. According to Dressler (1959), these basic and original principles include the following:

1. Offenders are reformable.
2. Reformation is the right of every convict and the duty of the state.
3. Every prisoner must be individualized. The emphasis would be on the offender, not the offense.
4. Time must be given the reformatory process to take effect.
5. The prisoner's cure is always facilitated by his cooperation and often impossible without it.
6. No other form of reward and punishment is so effective as transfer from one custodial class to another, with different privileges in each, but the most important agency for gaining a prisoner's cooperation is the power possessed by the administrators to lengthen or shorten the term of incarceration.
7. Finally, the reformatory process is educational. That means more than instructional. It includes the concept of re-education of attitudes, motivation, behavior.

Although the indeterminate sentence served as the forerunner to parole as it is known today, especially as the reformatory movement developed, parole legislation in the United States, and eventually in Canada, spread much more rapidly than the indeterminate sentence. In fact, the latter did not regain its popularity until well into the twentieth century and then mostly for youthful offenders.

Most early parole laws empowered state governors to attach conditions for early release from prison and gave wardens authority to violate technically those parolees who did not follow the terms and conditions of their release. The first statewide law pertaining to the parole of adults by an agent or agency other than the governor was passed in Ohio in 1884.

By 1901, twenty states had such parole laws, while only eleven states had indeterminate sentence laws. Eventually, every state passed a parole or aftercare (for juveniles) law, until some states decided to abolish parole in favor of determinate or fixed sentences.

Organization of Parole Systems

In the early days, parole decision making and administration were vested in the warden or superintendent of the correctional facility from which the inmate was released. As penal administration became more centralized, paroling power was transferred from individual institutions to state departments of correction.

Another trend was the creation of parole boards that are completely autonomous and independent of departments of correction—even though many are administratively attached to these departments for budgetary purposes. These boards are composed of members who must answer only to appointing authorities (usually governors). In this kind of organization, the paroling authority is responsible for decision making and policy setting, but the actual delivery of parole services (i.e., parolee supervision in the community) is generally administered by a separate field services agency, which frequently is part of a state department of correction.

A trend that overlaps the creation of parole boards is one in which a state authority, in the executive branch of government, combines probation and parole services and actually delivers such community-based services as well.

This trend toward centralization has been both defended and attacked because of the two distinct functions that parole involves: selection and supervision.

Selection of inmates paroled involves a range of decisions dealing not only with whom to parole and when to parole but with the effects of the release on the inmate, the institution, and the community. Supervision of paroled inmates involves a different range of decisions and responsibilities. These different responsibilities and functions must be recognized as underlying any discussion of parole administration (Korn & McCorkle 1965).

Role of the Parole Board

Although parole boards emerged over time as autonomous, decision-making authorities concerning the release of inmates, they also have taken on additional responsibilities as a consequence of gubernatorial requests or legislative mandates. These responsibilities include clemency, pardon, and commutation decisions and/or recommendations.

A pardon usually denotes "forgiveness" and can occur either before or after imprisonment. Constitutionally, only a chief executive (governor or president) can grant a pardon. However, a review for consideration for a pardon is frequently conducted by a parole board.

Clemency refers to the pardoning power of a chief executive for an inmate within the political jurisdiction. It may be initiated by the executive, but more often, an inmate files a formal petition with the executive, who then asks someone (frequently the parole board) to investigate the case and make appropriate recommendations. It is frequently used to correct unduly harsh sentences, for mitigating circumstances where guilt is dubious, for political reasons, or to avert the death penalty.

Commutation is an act of "mercy" by a chief executive that lessens the punishment of the original sentence, usually where imprisonment has been ordered. It is not significantly different from a pardon and has three main purposes: (1) to make eligible for parole those who were excluded from eligibility under their original sentence, (2) to make immediately eligible for parole those who are not yet eligible, and (3) to avoid the death penalty (Rubin 1973).

The Reduced Authority of Parole Boards

Since the 1970s, a new era in the role and utility of parole has emerged, namely its diminution or abolition. This has occurred as a result of increasing concerns for public safety, the politicization of criminal justice administration in general, rejection of rehabilitation as a primary goal of corrections, and lack of faith by the general public in the ability of parole (and other segments of criminal justice) to control offenders or otherwise reduce crime.

Rhine, Smith, and Jackson (1991) state that since the early 1970s, parole boards have been exposed to criticisms that are based on concerns about parole board decision making, discretion, and apparent lack of accountability. This criticism reflects, in part, disillusionment with indeterminate sentences, which basically serve as the foundation of the individualization of the offender. Rhine, Smith, and Jackson (1991) state:

> For a variety of reasons, most notably the politicization of crime control and the loss of faith in the ability of rehabilitative programs to effect offender change, jurisdictions across the country began to emphasize greater determinacy in sentencing. This drive was coupled with the passage of mandatory sentencing provisions, sentencing enhancements, and other measures designed to stiffen criminal penalties.

Sentencing codes in almost every state and the federal government have been revised, frequently replacing indeterminate sentencing with determinate sentencing and increasing the penalties for many offenses. Spurred by the U.S. Sentencing Commission, sentencing guidelines have been developed that require judges to make sentencing decisions according to mathematical formulas. Similarly, many states now have parole guidelines that govern board decision making concerning release. These guidelines, which are similar to probation classification systems, take into account the "risk" factors associated with the offender, including prior criminal history and likelihood for success in the community while under supervision. Rhine, Smith, and Jackson (1991) state the following:

> Even though no model [regarding codes or parole board discretionary authority for decision making] came to predominate, the impact on parole [of these changes], especially discretionary parole release, was dramatic. With Maine leading the way, between 1976 and 1979 six states either eliminated parole or severely limited parole release.... From 1980 to 1984 another five states followed suit...[and another abolished parole] as of 1980.... [However, between 1979 and 1985, at least three states have reinstated at least some form of parole or conditional release].

Notwithstanding assaults on parole in terms of its practice as well as its concept, it has been considered a significant part of the network of criminal justice services. As Rhine, Smith, and Jackson state, "...the legitimacy of parole, as well as the sentencing structure on which it rested, remained unquestioned.... Despite its diminishing role, discretionary parole release remains the primary method of release from confinement."

Conclusion

In recent years, there has been an increasing development of community-based corrections, including such programs as house arrest, day reporting, electronic monitoring, supervised pretrial release, restitution centers, and drug treatment programs. Notwithstanding these programmatic innovations, probation and parole not only remain the predominant forms of community-based corrections, they also tend to serve as the hosts for these other programs.

With the approach of the twenty-first century, the likelihood of increased resources to meet increasing caseload demands appears dim, and in fact further reductions in resources can be anticipated. This, of course, will occur even though court dockets and institutional commitments will continue to rise. Thus, probation and parole staffs will be expected to do more for larger numbers of offenders, but with diminished resources.

The task that lies ahead, then, is more goal-directed, systems-based management that looks to the future for better and different ways of accomplishing the correctional mission. This will also require a continuing assessment of programs and services to use available resources in the most effective and meaningful ways. And, finally, the successful implementation of community-based corrections—especially probation and parole—will require a greater partnership between communities and correctional organizations than ever before.

References

Allen, F. A. 1964. *The borderland of criminal justice.* Chicago: University of Chicago Press.

American Bar Association. 1974. *Standards relating to the administration of criminal justice.* Chicago: American Bar Association.

Cohn, A. W. 1970. We've got the whole caseload in our hands. *Popular Government* 36 (May): 17–21.

Cohn, A. W. 1976. *Crime and justice administration.* Philadelphia: J. B. Lippincott.

Cohn, A. W., and M. M. Ferriter. 1990. The Presentence investigation: An old saw with new teeth. *Federal Probation* LIV (September): 15–25.

Dressler, D. 1959. *Practice and theory of probation and parole.* New York: Columbia University Press.

England, R. W. 1957. What is responsible satisfactory probation and post-probation outcome? *Journal of Criminal Law & Criminology* 47:2–11.

Giardini, G. I. 1959. *The parole process.* Springfield: Charles C Thomas.

Grinnell, F. W. 1941. The common law history of probation. *Journal of criminal law and criminology* 32 (May-June): 15–34.

Killinger, G. C. 1951. Parole and services to the discharged offender. In *Contemporary correction,* ed. P. W. Tappan. New York: McGraw Hill.

Korn, R. R., and L. W. McCorkle. 1965. *Criminology and penology.* New York: Holt, Rinehart & Winston.

Lohman, J. D., A. Whal, and R. M. Carter. 1965–67. *The San Francisco project. Research reports 1–12.* Berkeley, Calif.: University of California.

Moran, F. A. 1945. The origins of parole. In *National Probation Association yearbook.* New York: NPA.

National Council on Crime and Delinquency. 1967. *Corrections in the United States.* Washington, D.C.: President's Commission on Law Enforcement and Administration of Justice.

Rhine, E. E., W. R. Smith, and R. W. Jackson. 1991. *Paroling authorities: Recent history and current practice*. Laurel, Md.: American Correctional Association.

Richmond, M. E. 1917. *Social diagnosis*. New York: Russell Sage Foundation.

Robison, J. 1969. *The California prison, parole and probation system: A special report to the Assembly*. Technical Supplement No. 2. Sacramento, Calif.: State of California.

Rubin, S. 1973. *The law of criminal correction*. 2d ed. St. Paul, Minn.: West Publishing Co.

Tappan, P. W. 1960. *Crime, justice and correction*. New York: McGraw-Hill.

Sutherland, E. H., and D. R. Cressey. 1970. *Criminology*. 8th ed. Philadelphia: J. B. Lippincott.

Turnbladth, W. C. 1956. Half justice. *National Probation and Parole Association Journal* 3:305–307

United Nations. 1951. The legal origins of probation. In *Probation and related measures*. New York: U. N. Department of Social Affairs.

U.S. Attorney General. 1939. *Attorney General's survey of release procedures—Vol IV*. Washington, D.C.: U.S. Government Printing Office.

APPLICABLE ACA STANDARDS

Standards for Adult Probation and Parole Field Services
  Personnel 2-3028
  Supervision—Probation and Parole Agencies 2-3155
  Supervision—Probation Agencies Only 2-3181, 2-3185

2

Presentence Investigation Reports

By Raymond Wahl

The presentence investigation (PSI) report is the basic working document courts use to determine appropriate sentences for offenders who have been convicted or who have pled guilty to criminal offenses.

PSI reports provide sentencing judges information relating to offenders. PSI reports serve the following functions (Administrative Office of the U.S. Courts 1978):

- help courts determine the appropriate sentence through providing timely, relevant, objective, and accurate data

- aid field officers in case management efforts

- aid institutions in their classification and programming efforts

- furnish releasing authorities pertinent information in their consideration of parole

- serve as a source of information for research

PSIs cover the defendant's life and characteristics and sometimes the informed recommendation of the field officer. In most instances, PSIs are conducted after the defendant has been found guilty or innocent. The field officer is not responsible for making these determinations.

Raymond Wahl is the director of Field Operations for the Utah Department of Corrections.

Content

The report given to the court may be verbal or written, long or short, but it always contains background information about the offender. Basic information such as date of birth, social security number, birth place, and parents' and siblings' names, can be helpful in obtaining records about the offender. Specific information about the circumstances of the arrest is important because a judge may have simply accepted a plea without knowing the actual details of the offense. The report should also note information about the victim and about any restitution owed.

The report contains information about the offender's prior record, both as an adult and juvenile. Dispositional information is important because convictions for past offenses are relevant to the court's consideration. Prior probation/parole supervision and performance is also relevant.

Additional information typically contained in a PSI report includes employment history, history of substance abuse and any treatment accessed, mental health condition and any treatment received, marital history, educational background, organizational or community affiliations, military record, and financial status. Much of the information in the PSI can be substantiated through contacts with family, friends, employers, treatment providers, law enforcement, and the prosecution.

Information in the report should be pulled together into a well-written evaluator's summary. In this summary, the field officer presents a professional assessment of the objective material in the report. The summary should contain an analysis of the facts that leads to a logical recommendation. The conclusion should be supported by the facts and represent their logical extension. The recommendation made by the agency must balance public safety and rehabilitation efforts.

Special Concerns

Victim Information

The victims movement of the 1970s spurred changes to the PSI format. Many states statutorily required a victim impact statement. For the field officer, the problem becomes the delicate balance of obtaining this information without opening up old wounds that may be healing. Many organizations obtain this information by mail, but a face-to-face interview should not necessarily be precluded. Specific information on the effect of the crime should be included. This information may be obtained from doctors, therapists, insurance companies, or the victims themselves. The field officer should act in an objective and professional manner when obtaining this information. (See Chapter 11, "Victims.")

Interview Techniques

Techniques used during the presentence process play an important role in obtaining information. Effective communication skills are needed to get offenders to reveal information about their lives and the offense that brought them before the court, thereby giving the court insight into the causes of the offense. The following are some suggested interview techniques:

1. Ask open-ended questions.

2. Practice reflective listening.

3. Try not to be judgmental.

4. Explain the sentencing process.

5. Don't make promises to the offender.

6. Be as objective as possible.

Writing Style

The field officer's job as an investigator is to communicate complex information in a logical and understandable report. The officer who has answered the questions who, what, when, where, why, and how can be fairly certain that he or she has a comprehensive report.

Legal Concerns

Officers should consult their legal advisors on issues specific to their jurisdiction's PSI report. However, there are some basic legal principles that can be applied to any PSI.

Contents. Because guilt or innocence has already been decided, PSIs allow judges wide discretion as to the sources, types of information, and credence placed on information. As a matter of due process and fundamental fairness, the defense counsel requires access to PSI reports. How this is accomplished, either by statute or policy, varies from jurisdiction to jurisdiction. However, courts have upheld the practice of excluding information from the report that reasonably could result in danger to the victim, collateral contact, or other party. Nonetheless, factors considered in arriving at the sentence will ultimately be accessible to at least the defendant's counsel.

Hearsay. Investigators may include hearsay (secondhand information) in PSIs, as long as it is identified as such. The discretion of the courts allows judges to place as much or as little emphasis on the information as they wish. These reports are not limited to the facts, but may include feelings, impressions, and conclusions that a source may have.

Disclosure. Generally, PSIs are disclosed to the defendant unless one of the following conditions exists:

1. Its release would disrupt the rehabilitation of the offender.

2. The information was obtained on a promise of confidentiality.

3. Release may result in harm to the defendant or others.

Many states have statutes, judicial rules, or policies that specify how the release of PSIs should be handled. The failure or refusal to disclose has not been a violation of the defendant's constitutional rights per se. Most arguments for release of PSIs revolve around the issue of "fundamental fairness"—that the defendant should have access to the PSI to be able to dispute inaccuracies and know the information relied on for the sentence imposed.

Preparing PSI Reports

This section is based on information from the Utah Department of Corrections Field Operations Manual (1988). Although the format presented here is but one of many used nationwide, it provides an idea of what is involved in preparing PSI reports.

Heading

The heading should provide significant identifying information regarding the offender, the court, and the specific case. The heading includes the following information:

- due date (the date the PSI is due to the court for review)

- sentence date (the date set by the court to sentence the defendant)

- name of the judge scheduled to sentence the defendant

- court with jurisdiction in the case

- city and county in which the case is being sentenced

- full name of the individual responsible for preparing the report

- name of the offender as shown on the court record

- other names or aliases by which the offender is known

- offender's address at the time of investigation

- offender's birth date, numerically by month, day, and year

- city and state, or country (if outside the United States) of the offender's birth

- offender's current legal residence

- current legal marital status of the offender (e.g., single, married, divorced, separated, widowed, or common-law)

- official court case numbers

- names of all co-defendants and defendants

Much of the field officer's time is spent writing reports and maintaining files.

- title and degree of the offense to which the offender has either pleaded guilty or has been found guilty

- statutory sentence for the offense(s)

- whether the defendant pleaded guilty or no contest or was convicted by trial and the date

- full name of the attorney(s) who prosecuted the case(s)

- full name of the offender's attorney or attorneys of record

- information regarding any plea bargaining, including any reduction of charges, dismissal of charges, charges not filed as a condition of the defendant pleading to the present charge, any arrangements regarding stipulations for the offender to make restitution in the current offense and other criminal episodes

Offense Section

Official Version. This is a summary or a direct copy of the police reports. Where a trial was not held, this is vital information for the sentencing judge.

Defendant's Version. The defendant's version should be included verbatim in the report. Additional questioning should be conducted when the statement is inadequate or the investigator has questions about the statement. When additional information is ascertained in an interview it may be presented to the courts as follows: "In addition to the written statement, the defendant in an interview with this investigator provided the following information."

If the offender does not provide a written statement, the investigator will interview the offender regarding his or her involvement in the crime and provide that information, documenting the time and place of the interview. Offenders should be questioned regarding activities leading to the offense, their motivation for committing the crime, what they hoped to gain, and attitudes about an appropriate sentence. To avoid misunderstandings, it is often best to repeat back to the offender his or her exact statement.

Co-defendant's Status. Provide a synopsis of the co-defendant(s) status, including court case numbers and notations on any dismissed cases, pending trials, pending sentencing, ninety-day diagnostic evaluations, or other psychological assessments on the co-defendant(s). Dates of these pending actions should be cited. If the co-defendants have been sentenced, that should be indicated along with the result of that sentencing. Court case numbers of the co-defendants should be used whenever possible.

Victim Impact Statement. The Victim Impact Statement should identify the victim of the offense; itemize any economic loss suffered by the victim as a result of the offense; identify any physical, mental, or emotional injuries suffered by the victim as a result of the offense, along with the seriousness and permanence; describe any change in the victim's personal welfare or familial relationships as a result of the offense; identify any request for mental health services initiated by the victim or the victim's family as a result of the offense; and contain any other information related to the effect of the offense on the victim or the victim's family.

Restitution. Restitution should be included in all offenses where a loss was sustained by the victim. Report the amount of loss relating to damage or stolen property, narcotics transaction, check forgeries, and for treatment (medical or psychological) received as a result of the current offense. Restitution as a part of any plea bargain negotiations must be addressed.

Custody Status. Report the time the offender was held in custody beginning with the date of arrest and ending with the release date on the offense being reported. This should include the number of days the offender was incarcerated

and the type of release (e.g., pretrial, property bond, or bail).

Prosecutor's Statement. This statement is made by the prosecutor in regard to the offender, the plea negotiations, the status of the case, and sentencing recommendation. The prosecutor is often able to provide details about the offense, the defendant, and the victims that may not be in the file.

Defense Attorney's Statement. This statement is made by the defense attorney regarding the offender, plea negotiations, status of the case, and sentencing recommendation.

Law Enforcement Statement. This is a statement by the arresting officer or an appropriate representative from the arresting agency for information regarding the arrest, the offender's attitude at the time of arrest, and the offender's cooperation since the time of the arrest.

Prior Record

Prior Record—Juvenile. Include all entries in the offender's juvenile record prior to the offender's eighteenth birthday. If no record exists, this should be documented.

Prior Record—Adult. Include all verifiable arrests of the offender subsequent to his or her eighteenth birthday. If no record exists, this should be documented.

Pending Cases. Determine if there are additional cases pending against the offender. The offense, degree, jurisdiction, and level of prosecution should be clearly outlined.

Probation/parole History. Include a synopsis of the offender's prior performance under probation or parole supervision. Significant problems previously encountered supervising the offender should be noted. If the offender has been supervised in another state, that state's information should be obtained if possible.

Background

Background Information and Present Living Situation. Background information properly obtained and evaluated may provide insight into the following areas:

- determination of the amount of support available to the offender from family members

- insight into the offender's attitude toward authority, community, social values, self-image, and lifestyle habits

- ability of the offender to adapt to groups and other social situations and circumstances

- cultural influences that affect the offender's beliefs and outlook regarding the offense committed and his or her role in the group, community, or society in general

The primary source for background information is the offender. Background information should have direct bearing on the offender's actions in present circumstances.

Marital History. As with background information, the primary source of information on the offender's marital history is the offender and his or her immediate family. Marital information may be verified through marriage licenses and divorce decrees. Absent this documentation, verification may be obtained through the county clerk or the court where the marriage license was issued or the divorce granted.

The investigator should evaluate the stability of the marital relationship, the effect the possible sentence may have on the relationship and the degree of support offered to the offender by the relationship.

The number of children and legal custody of children who resulted from the marriage or common law relationship should be listed in the marital status information. Where a divorce has been granted and the offender has been ordered to pay child support, the amount of child support ordered should be listed. Verification of child support obligations may be obtained through the clerk of the court where the divorce was granted. If the offender provides a divorce decree to verify the amount of child support ordered or the custody for minor children, the investigator must verify the order is the most current order issued by the court. Additional information may be obtained from family members, spouse, and/or former spouse(s).

Education. Indicate the highest grade completed, year, place, and reason for leaving school. Include subsequent education or vocational training. The best method of verification is a copy of the high school diploma and/or university degree.

The investigator should determine if there were any learning or behavioral problems during the educational process. The grades of the offender and his or her general attitude toward school are informative. Significant extra-curricular activities should be outlined. Special education classes or on-the-job training should be included. If the offender claims significant educational goals yet to be accomplished, they may be discussed.

Organizational or Community Affiliations. Focus on organizational affiliations (e.g., religious, professional, social) the offender feels has affected his or her life.

Health

Physical. Indicate the general health conditions of the offender. Include physical problems he or she may be experiencing, medication being used and the reasons for use, major hospitalization the offender has experienced and the causes of the hospitalization, and chronic or hereditary physical problems. Offenders may supply letters verifying medical history or may give written permission allowing their doctors to release privileged information.

Mental. Ask offenders why they feel their mental health is good or bad, if they view themselves as optimists or pessimists, how they handle themselves in stressful situations, how they feel about the present offense, and whether there is any history of mental health problems in their family. Indicate medication the offender has been placed on because of mental health problems. Give the specific name of medications and amount taken per day.

If the offender relates suicide attempts, details should be included. Note the events that led to the suicide attempt, the date of the attempt, and the mental health treatment the offender received as a result of these suicide attempts. The investigator should not attempt to diagnose the offender.

Substance Abuse

In addition to the initial presentence interview, police reports, prior arrest records, and available psychological information may also indicate substance abuse problems.

Employment History

List the history of the offender's employment beginning with the most recent job and include the following information:

- name of employer

- address of place of employment

- wage

- job title

- length of employment

- reason for leaving

Verification in the form of pay stubs, letters, etc., should be copied. The offender's prior employment history should be verified to the extent necessary to establish an employment pattern over several years. Former employers may also provide meaningful information concerning the offender. The offender's current employment must be verified. If the employer cannot or should not be contacted personally, the offender should be instructed to produce a letter from his or her immediate supervisor that documents dates of employment, job title, wage, and quality of work performance.

Financial Situation

Describe the offender's assets, income, and liabilities. The offender should furnish verification of these issues.

Military Record

Obtain significant military information regarding the offender. This information should include the dates of military service, the branch of the service, the highest rank obtained, the type of job performed, any disciplinary problems, and rank at discharge and the type of discharge. If the discharge is less than honorable, determine under what conditions the discharge was given.

Collateral Contacts

The purpose of the collateral contact is to collect pertinent and objective information for the court. Anyone who may verify existing information or provide additional information regarding the offender may be used.

Conduct the initial interview, read and compile collaborative information, then determine collateral contacts needed. The primary methods of collateral contacts will be through written correspondence or telephone contact.

Evaluative Summary

The evaluative summary may be the most demanding task of the PSI process. In the summary, the investigator presents a professional assessment of the objective material in the body of the report. The investigator must focus on those factors, social and personal, that result in the offender's presence before the court. The investigator must also consider the protection of the community along with the needs of the offender. The summary must not

simply repeat what has been presented, but rather analyze the facts leading to a logical recommendation.

The opening paragraph of this summary should give a concise restatement of the pertinent highlights of the body of the report.

The summary should continue by considering pertinent issues regarding the offender, the community, and finally the correctional system. Issues regarding the offender should include the following:

1. Was the offense situational or does it indicate an entrenched pattern of behavior that is likely to occur again?

Getting background information from family and acquaintances of offenders is important when preparing a presentence investigation report.

2. Was violence threatened or used?

3. Was a weapon involved?

4. Was the offense against a person or property?

5. What is the relative culpability between the defendant and co-defendants?

6. What was the motive for the offense?

7. What are the characteristics of the offender as they relate to relationships, behavior patterns, maturity, thinking and perception disorders, ability to relate to authority and society, and substance abuse?

8. What is the probability of the offender repeating the crime?

9. Does the offender accept responsibility for the crime?

10. Does the offender exhibit remorse for the crime or the victims?

11. Has the offender's behavior changed since the offense?

12. Is there a support system available for the offender?

The summary may continue by considering the following factors with regard to the community:

1. Is the community threatened by the offender?

2. How does the community view the crime?

3. What community resources are available regarding the treatment of the offender?

4. Would supervision actually be of any benefit to the offender or to society?

The final portion of the evaluative summary should include a review of the ability of the correctional system to appropriately deal with the offender. This review should take into account treatment resources available for the offender and special problems that would dictate the attention of institutional staff.

It is important that the conclusions reached in the evaluative summary be supported by facts and represent a logical extension of those facts. Aggravating and mitigating circumstances should be supported within the conclusion of the report. The agency recommendation should not be stated in the summary.

Investigator's Signature. The investigator who completes the report should sign it. The signature of the investigator indicates the information in the report is objective, reliable, current, and represents the best information available to the department of corrections.

Approval Signature. The approval signature indicates that the supervisor has reviewed and approved the report for form and content. The reliability, factual content, format, and recommendation are all certified as accurate and in accordance with department of corrections policy and procedure by this signature.

Conclusion

The PSI is the basic working document of the court during the sentencing phase. Recommendations made by officers can carry quite a bit of weight. Because of this, care must be taken to prepare the report in a professional, accurate, and timely matter to give the sentencing judge relevant and objective information on which to base sentencing. The trust the court places in the officer to prepare these reports should not be taken lightly.

References

Administrative Office of the United States Court, Division of Probation. 1978. *Presentence investigation report.* Washington, D.C.: GPO.

Utah Department of Corrections, Field Operations. 1988. *Presentence investigation report manual.* Salt Lake City: Utah DOC.

APPLICABLE ACA STANDARDS

Standards for Adult Probation and Parole Field Services
Supervision—Probation Agencies Only 2-3182
Presentence Investigation and Report 2-3185, 2-3188, 2-3190, 2-3195, 2-3200

3

Assessment and Supervision Planning

By Patricia M. Harris, Ph.D.

Intake is the first step of the community supervision process. It is the stage during which offender assessment and supervision planning uniformly occur, although reassessment and plan modification may take place later in supervision as well. Carefully executed assessments provide the foundation for positive officer-client relationships and effective supervision. When assessment and planning do not occur or are conducted poorly, supervision is haphazard, conducive to negative outcomes, and ultimately indefensible.

This chapter provides an overview of the intake process. It begins by describing the most commonly used assessments in probation and parole. Then it turns to a discussion of effective assessment interviewing protocol and technique. The chapter concludes with guidelines for developing an assessment-based supervision plan.

Information presented here on risk and needs assessment, the Client Management Classification system, and supervision planning reflects optimal community supervision intake procedures as recommended by the National Institute of Corrections. Needs and risk assessments like those discussed in this chapter are part of standard operating procedure in probation and parole agencies nationwide. The use of special needs assessments, such as the Substance Abuse Subtle Screening Inventory (SASSI), may differ from state to state and even from agency to agency within particular states. Within agencies, there

Patricia M. Harris, Ph.D., *is an assistant professor of criminal justice at the University of Texas at San Antonio.*

may be policies governing the types of cases (e.g., felony, high risk) for which more extensive assessments are required.

Risk Assessment

The purpose of risk assessment is to identify the level of supervision required by offenders entering probation or parole. Assessment entails completion of a questionnaire containing items such as number of prior convictions, age at first arrest, employment status, and drug or alcohol involvement. The items in risk scales are derived from empirical research that distinguishes between those who succeeded under community supervision and those who did not.

An example of a risk instrument developed for felony probationers in Texas is depicted in Figure 1. It has characteristics common to many risk assessment tools. Responses are structured (not open-ended), and different responses to the same item are given different weights. Note, for example, that no drug involvement in a previous year is assigned zero points and that any drug involvement is assigned four points. On completion of all items, the officer adds the points for a total risk score.

Overall risk scores represent a probability of supervision outcome, usually rearrest, over some subsequent period, such as three years. Table 1 displays projected probabilities of rearrest for probationers with different total risk scores obtained from the instrument depicted in

	Weighted Score
Figure 1. Felony Offender Risk Assessment (FORA)	

EMPLOYMENT status at assessment _____
    0   Employed (including student/retiree/disabled/homemaker)
    7   Unemployed

ALCOHOL problems in past year _____
    0   No problems indicated
    4   Problems indicated

Illicit **DRUG USE** in past year _____
    0   No Drug use indicated
    4   Drug use indicated

Total number of **PRIOR ARRESTS** _____
    0   No arrests
    2   One arrest
    4   Two to three arrests
    6   Four to five arrests
    8   Six or more arrests

Number of prior **FELONY CONVICTIONS** _____
    0   No convictions
    4   One or more convictions

AGE at assessment _____
    0   34 or older
    4   28 to 33
    8   24 to 27
   12   20 to 23
   16   17 to 19

INSTANT OFFENSE _____
    0   Nonproperty, nonperson
        (e.g. POCS, DWI, etc.)
    8   Offense against property
    7   Offense against person
        (including robbery)

ATTITUDE _____
    0   Motivated to change, receptive to assistance
    2   Somewhat motivated but dependent/unwilling to accept responsibility
    4   Rationalize behavior/negative/not motivated

Number of **PRIOR REVOCATIONS** (probation and/or parole) _____
    0   No prior revocations
    8   One or more

TOTAL _____

Table 1. Three-Year Outcomes Based on Felony Offender Risk Assessment Scores

Score	No. Rearrest (%)	Any Rearrest(%)	Personal Offense Rearrest (%)
0 – 3	96	4	0
4 – 8	86	14	3
9 – 13	85	15	1
14 – 18	70	30	4
19 – 23	61	39	6
24 – 28	49	51	6
29 – 33	41	59	11
34 – 38	37	63	11
39 – 43	28	72	11
44 – 49	23	77	21
50 – 55	22	78	23
56+	7	93	40

65 percent of the probationers were rearrested—many for very serious crimes, such as homicide, rape, aggravated assault, and robbery. Thus, the court erred sixty-five out of every hundred times it sentenced an offender to probation. The researchers asked if the court's success rate could be improved with a statistical risk instrument. They found that by basing the sentencing decision just on the conviction offense, the error rate could be cut to 44 percent. When prior criminal record and alcohol and drug use were taken into account, the error rate dropped to 33 percent. And when demographic characteristics, such as, age were included, the error rate dropped to 31 percent.

Officers sometimes wonder what the point is in performing risk assessment when it appears that much of the same information has already been gathered for the presentence investigation. Although it is true that both address many of the same subject areas, risk assessment differs from the presentence investigation in a crucial way. The items on risk assessments are weighted to signify the differential contribution particular characteristics make to the overall risk of reoffending posed by each individual offender. Thus, although both the presentence investigation and risk assessment include information on the offender's current employment status, only the risk assessment will weigh unemployment more or less heavily than other items.

The risk score is a very important piece of information to consider in case planning. At least twelve studies confirm that treatment efforts are more likely to produce positive effects when they are administered to offenders with high risk scores than when they are delivered to those with either medium or low risk scores (Andrews, Bonta & Hoge 1990). Moreover, many of these studies indicate that

Figure 1, for the first three years of supervision (Komala, Shepperd & Moczygemba 1990).

Much information typically required for risk assessment can be culled from the offender's case file. When officers ensure that the data they are using are current and accurate, risk instruments exhibit nearly perfect reliability—meaning that different officers will yield identical scores in the same cases. Some risk scales, however, contain items (e.g., attitude and involvement in drug or alcohol abuse) that necessitate consultation with the offender. Techniques for eliciting responses to these items are described in a later section.

Reliance on risk assessments over subjective judgments results in vastly improved predictions of recidivism. A study of 1,672 felons sentenced to probation in Los Angeles and Alameda counties in California illustrates just how dramatic the gain in accuracy can be (Petersilia et al. 1985). During an average follow-up of thirty-one months, application of treatment or other forms of intensive supervision to low-risk offenders results more frequently in negative outcomes than occurs when low-risk offenders are left alone.

Consequently, failure to take risk into account not only means diminished effectiveness of treatment for those who are in greatest need, it also means increased harm to those in least need. Of course, unless an agency has unlimited resources, it is impossible to provide intensive resources to all offenders. Services will undoubtedly be given to some and withheld from others. Unlike the prediction error that results when a low-risk offender is sentenced to prison, the prediction error that occurs when the high-risk probationer or parolee reoffends is a very visible one that could elicit unwanted negative public scrutiny of community corrections agencies. Thus, risk assessment provides a defensible basis for resource allocation.

Should an offender's risk score always be taken into account in planning supervision? The answer to this question is no—only because there will be a small percentage of offenders whose risk scores will be misleading. Imagine the risk score that would be incurred by a David Berkowitz (also known as Son of Sam) type of offender at the beginning of parole supervision. In light of his relatively advanced age at first commitment, absence of prior convictions, high education, and lack of prior probation or parole supervision (and therefore lack of revocations), Berkowitz would likely score very low on risk—yet pose possibly serious risks. Officers are advised to consider that risk assessments are developed from samples consisting of thousands of probationers and parolees who make up the bulk of the offenders they are likely to encounter on their caseloads on any given day. This means that in most cases, reliance on the risk score will yield a safer, sounder decision than would one's subjective judgment. However, departures from risk scores in excess of 25 percent of cases are ill-advised (Clear & Gallagher 1985).

Unfortunately, risk assessment instruments are frequently misused. The greatest misuse is no use at all (which could result either because no assessment is performed or because information from the assessment is not incorporated into case planning). However, there are other abuses that can occur even when assessment is conducted by officers harboring the best of intentions.

One problem is failure to employ a risk scale that has been validated on the population for which it is being used. Where items are identical, weights may differ across diverse populations. Items predictive of rearrest of probationers in one city or state may not be the items most predictive of rearrest in another. A study by Wright, Clear, and Dickson (1984) found, for example, that a risk instrument developed for Wisconsin probationers produced highly error-prone predictions when it was used on New York City cases. Further, items that are predictive of rearrest in probationers (e.g., prior revocations) may not be the same items that are predictive of rearrest in parolees (Clear & Gallagher 1985; Clear 1988).

Recently a risk assessment instrument that demonstrates greater resiliency across dissimilar populations has been introduced (Bonta & Montiuk 1992). The Level of Supervision Inventory (LSI), developed in Canada, yields predictions of acceptable accuracy in probationers, parolees, halfway house residents, and prison inmate populations. Moreover, risk predictions generated by the LSI are of greater accuracy than those obtained with more conventional assessments. The LSI requires a longer time to conduct, however, because it contains fifty-four items in comparison with the ten or so included in more traditional risk assessments.

A very different problem surrounds the use of cutoff scores to delineate low-, medium-, and high-risk cases. More often than not, cutoffs are standardized—meaning that the same scores are used to distinguish risk levels from year to year and even from agency to agency. Preset cutoffs are undesirable because of variation across agencies and over time with respect to what proportion of an agency's caseload will fall into each of the groups. Even if an agency were to divide its caseloads into three groups containing equal numbers of offenders, the number of cases falling into the high-risk category alone would likely exceed its budget for intensive services (Clear & Gallagher 1983). Labeling too many cases high risk on the basis of a preset cutoff can lead to too few resources being spread across too many cases. Community supervision officers and agencies are better advised to allocate services to their highest risk offenders, even if that means that some so-called high-risk individuals get supervised like the "mediums."

Officers should not lose sight of the reasons underlying a high-risk score. The cause of one offender's high-risk status may not be the cause of another's. High-risk scores do not automatically translate into a need for electronic monitoring, substance abuse treatment, or specialized supervision. Figuring out the reasons underlying an offender's risk of reoffending is the purpose of the needs assessment.

Needs Assessment

Needs assessment enables officers to determine areas in their clients' lives requiring intervention. Needs scales typically consist of items that assess the offender's status with respect to academic and vocational skills, employment, financial management, marital and family relationships, companions, emotional stability, alcohol and other drug use, physical health, and mental ability. Each item is measured along a four-point scale ranging from no problem in an area (considered a strength) to severe dysfunction. Higher total scores are indicative of greater need for intervention. A commonly used needs scale is depicted in Figure 2.

Unlike risk assessment, which relies extensively on objective information, needs assessment is very subjective. Reliability of responses to needs items across officers will depend mainly on the quality of each officer's interviewing skills and his or her ability to detect indicators of dysfunction, not merely from case records but from offenders' demeanor, speech, dress, and behavior patterns. In certain cases it may also be necessary to consult family members. Straightforward questions, such as simply asking an offender if he or she is emotionally unstable, are insufficient. Few individuals like to think of themselves this way. This manner of questioning is also limited because many offenders are either unaware that they have a problem or unaware of the extent of their problem.

There are numerous indicators of potential dysfunction for every needs area. For example, present offense (if it is income-producing), financial debt exceeding income, poor credit rating, frequent moves, poor math skills, chemical or gambling addictions, and disruption of utility services are all indicators of problems with financial management. Eliciting information that can help to determine existence of need sometimes requires asking offenders to complete a task. In assessing either academic skills or mental ability, for example, an officer might ask the offender to add together a few numbers (Community Justice Assistance Division 1991a).

Agencies often use more sophisticated tools in addition to the general assessment in determining need for offender interventions. The Client Management Classification (CMC) system tends to be used with high-risk versus low-risk offenders, but may be used to assess any offender population. Special needs assessments may also be used to screen for dysfunction in particular problem areas.

Client Management Classification

The CMC process involves a semistructured interview that elicits detailed information from the offender about his or her involvement in the immediate offense, offense pat-

terns, school adjustment, vocational and residential adjustment, family attitudes, interpersonal relations, emotions, plans, and attitude toward supervision. It also takes note of some objective background information and the officer's subjective assessment of factors like the offender's grooming, affect, and cooperation into account. CMC scores permit the officer to place the offender being interviewed into one of five classifications, also known as strategy groups. The groups consist of limit setting, environmental structure, casework/control, selective intervention (treatment), and selective intervention (situational) offenders. Once offenders are classified, manner of officer/client interaction, supervision goals, type and number of referrals, and strategies for responding to violations of supervision conditions are shaped by the particular group in which each offender falls.

Limit-setting offenders embody characteristics conventionally attributed to offenders. They have a firm criminal value orientation, commit crimes to serve materialistic and self-serving desires, and commonly disregard the needs of others. These offenders possess good social skills that enable them to manipulate others.

Environmental structure offenders are characterized by impulsivity. They are often very naive and gullible, and they commit crimes either because they have been duped by others or because they strive to be accepted by others. These offenders frequently lack social, vocational, and general survival skills.

Casework/control offenders exhibit a chaotic and unstable life pattern. They have poor attitudes toward authority, have low self-esteem, are failure-oriented, and lack goal directedness. They tend to be among the most frustrating of offenders to supervise, because their high capability is in such marked contrast to their frequently negative performance. Casework/control offenders may have long-standing emotional problems stemming from unstable childhoods, as well as chemical dependency.

Selective intervention offenders differ from either casework/control or limit setting offenders because of their social value system. Unlike the environmental structure offender, they are also very capable. Selective intervention (treatment) offenders exhibit a single treatment need stemming from either chemical abuse, assaultiveness, sexual deviancy, or an emotional problem, such as depression. Selective intervention (situational) offenders consist of very low-risk, first-time offenders whose involvement in crime is due to isolated factors unlikely to be repeated.

The CMC is a powerful tool. Several carefully executed evaluations have found that differentially supervised offenders are far less likely to violate the terms of

Figure 2. Needs Assessment	**Score**

1 ACADEMIC/VOCATIONAL SKILLS _____
- -1 High school or above skill level
- 0 Adequate skills; able to handle everyday requirements
- +2 Low skill level causing minor adjustment problems
- +4 Minimal skill level causing serious adjustment problems

2 EMPLOYMENT _____
- -1 Satisfactory employment for one year or longer
- 0 Secure employment; no difficulties reported; or homemaker, student, or retired
- +3 Unsatisfactory employment or unemployed but has adequate job skills
- +6 Unemployed and virtually unemployable; needs training

3 FINANCIAL MANAGEMENT _____
- -1 Long-standing pattern of self-sufficiency; e.g., good credit
- 0 No current difficulties
- +3 Situational or minor difficulties
- +5 Severe difficulties; may include overdrafts, bad checks, or bankruptcy

4 MARITAL/FAMILY RELATIONSHIPS _____
- -1 Relationships and support exceptionally strong
- 0 Relatively stable relationships but potential for improvement
- +3 Some disorganization or stress
- +5 Major disorganization or stress

5 COMPANIONS _____
- -1 Good support and influence
- 0 No adverse relationships
- +2 Associations with occasional negative results
- +4 Associations almost completely negative

6 EMOTIONAL STABILITY _____
- -2 Exceptionally well-adjusted; accepts responsibility for actions
- 0 No symptoms of emotional instability; appropriate functioning
- +4 Symptoms limit, but do not prohibit adequate functioning; emotional responses, e.g., excessive anxiety
- +7 Symptoms prohibit adequate functioning; e.g., lashes out or retreats into self

7 ALCOHOL USE PROBLEMS _____
- 0 No use; use with no abuse; no disruption of functioning
- +3 Occasional abuse; some disruption of functioning
- +6 Frequent abuse; serious disruption of functioning

8 OTHER DRUG USE PROBLEMS _____
- 0 No disruption of functioning
- +3 Occasional abuse; some disruption of functioning
- +5 Frequent abuse; serious disruption of functioning

9 MENTAL ABILITY _____
- 0 Able to function independently
- +3 Some need for assistance; potential for adequate adjustment; possible retardation
- +6 Deficiencies severely limit independent functioning; possible retardation

10 HEALTH _____
- 0 Sound physical health; seldom ill
- +1 Handicap or illness interferes with functioning on a recurring basis
- +2 Serious handicap or chronic illness; needs frequent medical care

11 SEXUAL BEHAVIOR _____
- 0 No apparent dysfunction
- +3 Real or perceived situational or minor problems
- +5 Real or perceived chronic or severe problems

PO's IMPRESSION OF PROBATIONER'S NEEDS _____
- -1 Well adjusted
- 0 No Needs
- +3 Moderate Needs   **TOTAL NEEDS SCORE** _____
- +5 High Needs   **NEEDS LEVEL** _____

their supervision than those who are not differentially supervised. A 1979 study that compared three offender groups consisting of regularly supervised, intensively supervised, and both intensively and differentially supervised probationers found that probationers who were both intensively and differentially supervised experienced lower rates of revocation, higher rates of full-time employment, and higher rates of income over $400 per month than were either the regularly supervised or intensively supervised groups (Lerner, Arling & Baird 1986).

A study conducted by the Texas Board of Pardons and Paroles compared the effects of differential and regular supervision across high-, medium-, and low-risk groups (Eisenberg & Markley 1987). An analysis of prerevocation warrant rates at one year found substantially higher warrant rates for regularly supervised high- and medium-risk cases than for cases of similar risk who were differentially supervised. For example, among regularly supervised high-risk parolees, the warrant rate was one in three, but it was only one in four for those who were supervised according to particular strategy groups. There was no difference in warrant rates across regularly and differentially supervised low-risk groups. These findings underscore the importance of taking both risk and needs into account in community supervision.

A comparison of 419 offenders supervised by the North Carolina Department of Probation, Parole and Pardon Services found dramatic differences in rates of return to prison across CMC and non-CMC supervised offenders. The rate of return for offenders who were supervised according to the CMC was only 14.6 percent, compared with 38 percent for those not supervised according to the CMC (McManus, Stagg & McDuffie 1988).

Officers are sometimes intimidated by the forty-five minutes required to conduct a valid CMC assessment, but this apprehension is unfounded. When a CMC is completed, both the risk and needs assessments can be scored very quickly. The depth provided by the CMC in such areas as attitude, emotions, and substance abuse means greater accuracy of response to similar items appearing on either the risk or needs assessments and greater reliability in scoring as cases pass from officer to officer. Practice of differential supervision according to the CMC means less time spent later in an offender's supervision documenting and filing on violations.

Special Needs Assessments

Criminal justice agencies sometimes use special instruments for assessing whether or not an offender is chemically abusive or dependent and for determining nature and extent of sexual deviancy. Commonly used substance abuse instruments include the Mortimer-Filkins Interview and Questionnaire, the Substance Abuse Subtle Screening Inventory (SASSI), and the Addiction Severity Index (ASI). The Multiphasic Sex Inventory (MSI) is one commonly used tool for assessing offenders with known or suspected sexual offending.

The Mortimer-Filkins is used only to assess extent of problem drinking (versus other types of chemical abuse). It sorts subjects into social, presumptive problem, and problem-drinker categories. The assessment contains two parts, an officer-administered interview and a self-report questionnaire, with the former weighted more heavily than the latter. The interview takes about thirty minutes. The self-report consumes an additional fifteen. The blood alcohol content and driver and criminal records tally sheet enables officers to sort presumptive problem drinkers into either social-or problem-drinker categories. Because the Mortimer-Filkins probes dysfunction in the area of physical and mental health, relationships, finances, and employment, it can serve as a basis for determining what other referrals in addition to alcohol treatment may be needed (Kerlan et al. 1971).

The SASSI detects both drug and alcohol dependency. It sorts respondents into nonabuser, honest abuser, and faking abuser categories—thus, it permits identification of alcohol and drug abuse even among those in denial. Scores of the SASSI can be used to measure type of abuse (alcohol versus drug), as well as extent. Officers can use its results to determine whether inpatient or outpatient treatment is appropriate (Miller 1985). One of its main advantages is its self-report format, which takes approximately ten minutes for the offender to complete and one minute for the officer to score. It does not, however, provide information on any other needs a particular offender may have.

The ASI consists of a thirty- to forty-five-minute interview that provides measures of a respondent's dysfunction in each of six treatment areas, including drug and alcohol abuse, medical condition, psychological health, legal involvement, family/social functioning, and employment/support status (McLellan et al. 1980). Unlike the SASSI, the ASI places addiction in the context of factors that either contribute to or result from substance abuse. The ASI's ten-point scale provides officers with estimates of problem severity.

The MSI, a comprehensive self-report questionnaire, classifies subjects by deviance type and measures respondents' levels of sexual deviance on numerous scales (including rape, child molestation, and exhibitionism). It also measures sexual dysfunction, sexual knowledge, and

Offenders are more likely to disclose accurate and relevant information when they feel at ease with their probation or parole officers. *(Officer on the left.)*

ment, officers should verify each offender's ability to read and comprehend items if a meaningful assessment is to be obtained. This can be verified by asking the offender to read a few items aloud and paraphrase their meaning.

Assessment Interviewing

The quality of any assessment depends on the officer's ability to get the offender to disclose accurate and relevant information. Disclosure can effectively be accomplished when officers practice appropriate interviewing skills. These skills include making the offender feel at ease, asking appropriate questions in a nonthreatening manner, listening carefully to what is said and not said, and making correct interpretations from the information that is elicited. This section on assessment interviewing is based on the Community Justice Assistance Division's *Strategies for Case Supervision Training Manual* (1991b) and the work of Halley, Knopp, and Austin (1992).

Many officers greet the idea that an offender can be helped to disclose personal and sensitive information—even information that is potentially damaging to his or her case—with skepticism. In such cases, the offender's failure to disclose is less a function of the inability or unwillingness of the offender to cooperate than it is a function of the officer's inability to relate to the offender. When conducting assessments, officers should convey authority in the sense of confidence, not power.

attitudes toward treatment (Nichols & Molinder 1984). Generally, offenders are referred out to clinicians for MSI assessment.

In selecting special assessment tools, instruments that present both acceptable levels of validity and ease of administration and scoring are preferred. Instruments that contain mainly face validity items (e.g., items that obviously probe drinking and drug use) will likely fail to ascertain drug and alcohol problems in offenders who are experiencing denial. In contrast, instruments with many criterion validity items (e.g., items that probe behavior known to be associated with alcohol or drug problems) effectively penetrate denial in many respondents. The best instruments will contain face valid items for the purpose of assessing denial only. When using a self-report instru-

Making the offender feel at ease means establishing rapport with the offender and communicating a sincere interest in him or her. Assessments should begin with a handshake and brief small talk. For example, the officer might inquire whether the offender had any difficulty finding the probation or parole office. The officer should then explain the purpose of the interview. Rather than preventing the offender from opening up, as is conventionally assumed, informing offenders how their time will be used conveys to them that they are worthy. This in turn fosters communication.

Rapport is enhanced by matching verbal and nonverbal behavior. Verbal matching occurs when speed, volume, and tone of voice are similar. The officer should avoid responding to an offender's soft and slow speech with rapid and loud utterances, or vice versa. Officers should refrain from sounding mechanical while conducting interviews. Nonverbal matching calls for congruence of breathing and posture, within reason. Officers should never mimic the actions of the offender.

Both verbal and nonverbal matching can be used to make the offender more receptive. For example, an officer whose client is speaking in a slow, depressed speech should initially match volume and speed and then gradually increase both. The tendency of parties in an interview to adapt to the behavior patterns of their partners underscores the need for officers to remain aware of the effect their own posture and verbal behavior can have on the interview process. Officers who are stiff and mechanical will probably elicit similar behavior in their clients.

Interviewers should maintain good eye contact, sit facing the offender, and reflect a relaxed and open posture (e.g., arms should not be crossed). Officers should never turn their backs on their clients while the interview is taking place.

Successful assessment interviews depend on the officer's ability to ask pertinent questions in an appropriate manner. An important part of effective questioning is suspending judgment. Suspending judgment means not imposing stereotypes. One common stereotype is the belief that all offenders are liars. This does not mean that officers should accept everything the offender says at face value. It *does* mean that the officer should wait for the offender to finish responding before tactfully probing the validity of his or her account.

Suspending judgment also means avoiding questions that begin with the word "why." These type of questions convey criticism and can cause the offender to withdraw. Officers should also avoid expressions of alarm, indignation, disgust, or amusement, no matter how outrageous the account being given. Behaving as if the story being told is perfectly reasonable and normal enhances communication. It is sometimes useful, however, to express emotions where those expressions convey empathy for what is being said.

Generally speaking, open-ended questions are preferable to close-ended questions. Offenders who are asked yes or no questions will respond with a yes or no and fall silent. Instead of asking whether an offender feels remorseful about involvement in a particular offense, it is better to inquire how he or she felt. Rather than asking offenders whether they are addicted to drugs, it is preferable

to ask them to describe a typical week of drinking or drug use. Sometimes assessments specify that particular questions be asked in a certain way; officers should pay careful attention to instructions regarding how particular items are to be delivered. When open-ended questions are used, subjects should be allowed to fully respond before the interviewer moves on to another question.

Officers should listen carefully for statements that are ambiguous or in contradiction with some earlier statement. They should ask follow-up questions in a non-threatening manner to resolve inconsistencies or clarify ambiguities. They should frequently reflect back to the offender what has been said, to make sure that the offender's intended meaning has been conveyed. They should also listen for what is *not* said. For example, the officer should probe sudden changes in nonverbal behavior, and follow-up on answers that appear to be distortions, deletions, or generalizations of the truth.

Sometimes an offender will fail to respond or will provide an answer that is obviously inappropriate. In these instances the officer should determine whether the offender understands the questions being asked. The officer should not assume that the offender is being insolent. If the offender does not understand, the officer should begin to use simpler language. Officers should also be sensitive to the fact that many offenders are not fluent in English. When the offender does not have a sufficient understanding of English, assessments should be conducted by officers who are fluent in the offender's native tongue.

Sometimes offenders refuse to participate with the assessment. Instead of forcing the interview, the officer should attempt to build rapport around the resistance by empathizing with the offender's frustration or anger. It is sometimes possible to build enough rapport to proceed with the interview.

Unless the offender is exhibiting signs of crisis, officers should avoid counseling and advising the offender. Assessment interviews are about eliciting information; they should not be used as an information exchange.

Offices or other settings where assessment is to take place should be clean, uncluttered, and private. Ample time should be set aside to allow for a valid assessment. Officers should hold their phone calls and otherwise discourage interruptions while the interview is taking place. Interruptions break rapport and communicate to the offender that he or she is unworthy. Officers should close their interviews by thanking the offender for his or her time.

Supervision Planning

Once assessment is complete, the officer should prepare a supervision plan based on the information gained from the risk and needs interviews. This section on supervision planning is based on the work of Gingerich (1991a, 1991b & 1991c).

Supervision planning is an essential step in the intake process. Unfortunately, planning is often hastily conducted, resulting in neglect of assessment results. Failure to rely on the information gained at assessment is one reason some officers resent devoting time to this phase of supervision. Those who fail to take the steps to implement assessment-based supervision never encounter its benefits for the system and the offender.

There are many good reasons for drawing up a supervision plan (in addition to the fact that plans are usually required in probation and parole agencies). Formal plans increase success of community supervision. Plans enhance the efficiency of field officers by keeping them "on track." The supervision plan clarifies expectations of supervision. It lets the offender know exactly what is expected of him or her. A plan represents shared ownership: Because the planning process solicits the offender's participation, he or she will have a stake in carrying out the plan. A plan protects the officer by limiting liability in the event the probationer or parolee reoffends. Without a plan, the officer will be hard-pressed to explain why certain actions were taken in a case and why others were not.

There are four steps in the planning process: force-field analysis, problem prioritization, plan composition, and plan negotiation.

Force-field Analysis

Force-field analysis is a brief social history of the offender that is completed by the officer immediately following administration of the CMC. A completed force-field analysis will reflect two important pieces of information for each of the areas highlighted in the general needs assessment: a summary of the offender's resources in a particular needs area and a summary of his or her weaknesses in that area. An example of a weakness in a particular offender's case is three prior convictions of driving while intoxicated (DWI). An example of a matching strength is that he or she has maintained sobriety for four months. The force-field analysis is not only a useful reminder of the most salient features of an offender's life learned in an assessment, it is the basis for prioritizing and targeting areas of need to be addressed by supervision.

Problem Prioritization

Problem areas require prioritization because offenders often have many problems, and prospects for addressing all of them or all of them at one time within the range of resources and duration of supervision available are often low. When ranking problems, the officer takes each of the following four criteria into account: the extent to which the problem contributes to the offender's involvement in crime; whether or not the problem is alterable; how quickly the offender is able to act on the problem; and the relation, or interdependence, of the problem to other areas of need.

For example, alcohol abuse would be regarded as a contributor to criminal behavior if the offender became assaultive when he or she consumed alcohol. It would not be so regarded if on getting drunk, the offender went to bed and slept it off. That is not to say that the alcohol abuse is not a problem, only that it does not directly contribute to involvement in crime. Problems such as very low intelligence generally cannot be fixed by probation supervision and so should be regarded as unalterable. An offender might benefit tremendously from vocational training, but if there is a six-month wait for new admissions where the training is given, vocational deficits cannot be quickly fixed. Also, poor financial management that contributes to adverse marital or family relationships can be considered an interdependent problem.

Unless the offender has very few problems, only problem areas that exhibit all four characteristics are then considered. If there are several such areas, the officer ranks them by the order in which they will be addressed.

Plan Composition

After problems are ranked, the officer is ready to create a supervision plan. A plan contains four parts: a problem statement, behavioral objectives, an offender action plan, and an officer action plan.

Problem statements indicate which specific behaviors get the offender in what particular kinds of trouble. They link undesirable behaviors with undesirable consequences.

Behavioral objectives, perhaps the most important part of the plan, state specifically what behaviors the offender should engage in to avoid further experiencing the difficulties noted in the problem statement. For an assaultive offender, an example of one appropriate behavioral objective is attending an anger management class. Effective objectives are realistic, time-framed (e.g., results should be observable over some finite period of time, such as the following six months), and positively stated.

Offender action plans specify how the offender will carry out the behavioral objective (e.g., what program he or she will attend, frequency of attendance, and for how long). Officer action plans, on the other hand, specify what assistance the officer will give to the offender and what methods he or she will use to verify that the offender is carrying out his or her obligations.

Plan Negotiation

Supervision planning finishes with negotiation. Although some officers may balk at the idea of a give-and-take with the offender in supervision planning, the payoffs are substantial. Research indicates that negotiated plans yield higher rates of compliance with conditions of supervision than do plans that have not engaged offender participation (Clear 1977). Negotiated plans are more successful because they empower offenders and give them a stake in the outcome. They are also more effective because they provide the officer with a "reality check": the officer learns before it is too late what aspects of the plan the offender can practically fulfill and which he or she cannot. Negotiated plans do not result in the abdication of important behavioral objectives; after all, the officer is a party to the negotiation as well. Offenders who refuse to agree to attend substance abuse counseling, for example, can be reminded of less desirable alternatives, such as revocation. Once the plan is negotiated, both officer and offender sign the agreement. This completes the intake process.

Case classification does not end at intake. Offenders are reclassified by their officers on both risk and needs status at regular intervals (e.g., every six months). Reclassification provides a way to evaluate client progress and to ensure that supervision and referral resources are being used where they are most needed.

Conclusion

Efficient use of limited community supervision resources requires both careful administration of risk and needs assessments and thoughtful incorporation of assessment results in case planning. Good interviewing skills, including avoidance of nonthreatening behaviors on the part of the officer, are needed to elicit offender cooperation. Following assessment, allocation of resources should favor higher risk cases if maximum impact on low-violating behaviors is to be achieved.

References

Andrews, D. A., J. Bonta, and R. D. Hoge. 1990. Classification for effective rehabilitation: rediscovering psychology. *Criminal Justice and Behavior* 17:19–52.

Bonta, J., and L. L. Montiuk. 1992. Inmate classification. *Journal of Criminal Justice* 20:343–53.

Clear, T. R. 1977. *The specification of behavioral objectives in probation and parole.* Unpublished Ph.D. dissertation, State University of New York at Albany.

———. 1988. Statistical prediction in corrections. *Research in Corrections* 1:1–52.

Clear, T. R., and K. W. Gallagher. 1983. Screening devices in probation and parole: Management problems. *Evaluation Review* 7:217–34.

———. 1985. Probation and parole supervision: A review of current classification practices. *Crime and Delinquency* 31:423–43.

Community Justice Assistance Division. 1991b. *Training manual in case classification.* Austin, Tex.: Texas Department of Criminal Justice.

———. 1991a. *Strategies for case supervision training manual.* Austin, Tex.: Texas Department of Criminal Justice.

Eisenberg, M., and G. Markley. 1987. Something works in community supervision. *Federal Probation* 51:28–32.

Gingerich, R. 1991a. *Introduction to supervision planning: Force field.* Austin, Tex.: Community Justice Assistance Division.

———. 1991b. *Problem prioritization.* Austin, Tex.: Community Justice Assistance Division.

———. 1991c. *Writing the plan.* Austin, Tex.: Community Justice Assistance Division.

Halley, A. A., J. Knopp, and M. J. Austin. 1992. *Delivering human services.* New York: Longman.

Kerlan, M. W., et al. 1971. *Court procedures for identifying problem drinkers Volume I—Manual.* Ann Arbor, Mich.: University of Michigan.

Komala, M., V. D. Shepperd, and M. L. Moczygemba. 1990. *The felony offender risk assessment study: Progress report.* Austin, Tex.: Community Justice Assistance Division.

Lerner, K., G. Arling, and S. C. Baird. 1986. Client management classification strategies for case supervision. *Crime and Delinquency* 32:254–71.

McLellan, A. T., et al. 1980. An improved diagnostic evaluation instrument for substance abuse patients: The addiction severity index. *Journal of Nervous and Mental Disease* 168:26–33.

McManus, R. F., D. I. Stagg, and C. R. McDuffie. 1988. CMC as an effective supervision tool: The South Carolina perspective. *Perspectives* (Summer): 30–34.

Miller, G. A. 1985. *The substance abuse subtle screening inventory* manual. Spencer, Ind.: Spencer Evening World.

Nichols, H. R., and I. Molinder. 1984. *Multiphasic sex inventory manual*. Tacoma, Wash.: Nichols and Molinder.

Petersilia, J., et al. 1985. *Granting felons probation: Public risks and alternatives*. Santa Monica, Calif.: Rand.

Wright, K. N., T. R. Clear, and P. Dickson. 1984. Universal applicability of probation risk-assessment instruments. *Criminology* 22:113–34.

APPLICABLE ACA STANDARDS

Standards for Adult Probation and Parole Field Services
Supervision 2-3105, 2-3110, 2-3114, 2-3116, 2-3120
Supervision—Parole Agencies Only 2-3167
Supervision—Probation Agencies Only 2-3184

4

Supervision of Probationers

By William D. Burrell

There are hundreds of probation agencies in the United States. Each operates under the unique laws, traditions, and practices of each state and the federal government. Even within states there is likely to be operational variation, because many probation agencies are county-based.

The information in this chapter represents a distillation of practices of many jurisdictions and sets forth the basics of contemporary probation practice in the United States.

Supervision and the Role of the Officer

Probation supervision is the process of monitoring the activities and behavior of a convicted offender and providing assistance and services to help bring about behavioral changes. An essential part of monitoring and assistance is the enforcement of court-ordered requirements.

In defining probation in this way, there are several core functions for probation and several roles for the probation officer to play.

William D. Burrell is chief of Supervision Services in the Probation Services Division, Administrative Office, of the New Jersey Courts.

The Role of Probation

Probation has many roles. Two of the major roles are surveillance and services. The basic distinction between the two roles is the probation officer as a watchdog and the officer as a helper.

The surveillance role of probation has also been referred to as the monitoring, police, law enforcement, or controlling role. In this role, probation officers watch probationers to see if they are complying with the conditions of probation. When it appears that they are not in compliance, some sort of action is taken. In this role, the action taken in response to noncompliance is usually punitive, such as the filing of violation-of-probation charges or, at the extreme, the arrest and detention of the probationer.

This role emphasizes the crime control aspect of probation, where the officer functions much like an extension of the police. The goal is to discover noncompliant behavior and then respond with some type of sanction. This sanction serves to notify the probationer that this particular behavior is not acceptable and thus to deter the probationer from engaging in similar behavior in the future.

In contrast to the surveillance role, the services role of probation emphasizes providing assistance to the probationer in meeting the requirements of the court order and in achieving positive personal and social adjustments through behavior change. The role is also known as the social work, counselor, helping, assistance, or rehabilitation role of probation. In this role, services or access to services that can help the probationer make needed behavioral changes are provided.

The services role of probation has its roots in the rehabilitative purposes of sentencing. In many instances, it is possible to identify personal characteristics and behaviors or social interaction patterns that contribute either directly or indirectly to criminal behavior. If these behaviors can be altered or eliminated, it is more likely that the criminal behavior can be eliminated as well.

If they are defined very narrowly, the surveillance and services roles can form a clear dichotomy. The probation officer is either a "cop" or a counselor, but not both, some have argued. All types of problems, from unclear organizational mission statements to probation officer burnout, have been laid at the feet of this role conflict. An organization that is unsure of its role is unlikely to be very effective.

This controversy provides an opportunity to clarify the role of probation and indeed to expand it to some degree. Through this process, a more accurate and more useful model for the role of probation emerges.

Field probation officers often dismiss this role conflict as not reflecting the real work of the probation officer. Their response is, "We are both 'cops' and counselors. It depends on the case and it depends on the time. Sometimes you do one and at other times, you do the other. It depends on what you are trying to accomplish."

This reflects the practical requirement to pursue the two roles. Pursuit of one without a balance of the other departs from probation's unique role and in fact will reduce effectiveness. A probation officer who just monitors probationers and sanctions them for noncompliance is missing the significance of problems and needs that are contributing to criminal behavior. Simply monitoring and sanctioning without addressing the underlying problems will only return offenders to court and possibly to jail. The opportunity to intervene and stop the cycle of criminality is lost.

Similarly, an officer who pursues just the services role is ignoring legal enforcement responsibilities and is not making use of the court's authority and the probationer's conditional liberty status as a motivating force for behavioral change.

The probation officer's role is unique. That uniqueness flows from the dual nature of the sentence to probation, which has both rehabilitative and punitive purposes. As the agents appointed to carry out this sentence, probation officers must incorporate both purposes into their role.

Integrating these roles into a new one provides an opportunity to better define the probation profession, to give a clearer vision of its role and responsibilities and its place in the criminal and juvenile justice systems. Rather than trying to force a fit of probation into someone else's role, a new role needs to be synthesized, articulated, and put into place.

A New Definition of the Role of Probation

Searching for the "bottom line" in any endeavor usually provides guidance about what is really important, what really has to be done. In probation, it can be argued that the bottom line is enforcement of the court's order. When all is said and done, the probation officer and the probation organization should be held accountable for enforcing the court order. Compliance with the court order is crucial, and when that is not forthcoming, some action must be taken.

This enforcement paradigm provides added flexibility for consideration of the role of probation. It can incorporate both of the traditional roles (surveillance and services) as well as new roles or variations on existing ones that may emerge as the field of probation matures and evolves.

The probation officer is responsible for enforcing the court's order. In that order, the judge sets forth expectations for the probation supervision process. Depending on the individual order, these expectations may be punitive, rehabilitative, incapacitative, retributive, or a combination of several. Carrying out supervision to meet these expectations may require probation officers to engage in surveillance, service, or other activities. They may be pursued in combination or alone, and differing activities may be done by the officer on the same case at differing points in time.

Probation officers are responsible for determining what is to be done in carrying out the court's order, how to do it, and when to do it. The court sets forth the basic expectations and vests the probation officer with the authority and discretion to make the decisions about how to meet the expectations. Although there are basic principles and proven techniques probation officers can refer to, the specifics of where, when, and how to apply them are decisions that can only be made by the officer on a case-by-case basis.

The Focus of Probation

Probation officers have their duties and responsibilities, but so do probationers. At times it may seem as though probationers are trying to turn the table on officers by challenging them to find unemployed probationers jobs or drug abusers treatment. Probation officers can help, but they cannot change an unwilling probationer. The responsibility to abide by the conditions of probation must be placed squarely on the shoulders of the probationer.

The Supervision Process

The probation supervision process is a complex set of interactions among the probation officer, the probationer, other criminal justice and social service agencies and organizations, and the community at large. Although each case is unique to some degree, it is still possible to discuss the common elements of the supervision process. These are the basic steps taken by a probation officer in designing and carrying out supervision.

Initial Assessment

When a case is first received for supervision, the probation officer performs an assessment (see Chapter 3). Depending on individual agencies this can be formalized

and structured or left up to individual officers to handle as they see fit. Whatever the degree of formality, certain decisions are made.

The first is to review the requirements set forth in the court order. Often, the court will require substance abuse treatment or other services, which the probation officer will have to arrange.

Next, the officer will have to get more familiar with the case. This is done through a review of the presentence report and other court records and reports and in an interview or series of interviews with the probationer. Officers commonly visit the probationer's home and possibly other places in the community, such as place of employment.

Probation officers seek to identify the problems and needs of probationers. These may be a part of the conditions of probation, they may contribute to continuing illegal behavior, or they may interfere with the officer's attempts to help the probationer comply with the court order. Because one of the purposes of probation is rehabilitation, or changing problematic behavior, a thorough assessment and understanding of the probationer's problems and needs is essential to formulating and carrying out an effective supervision strategy.

With this information in hand, the probation officer can begin to make some decisions about the case and its supervision requirements.

Supervision Priority

Probation officers decide the priority of the cases for supervision. Which cases must receive first priority and most supervision? Which cases can be given less? Officers must decide how to allocate their time among their cases.

This is not just a practical matter, in terms of managing limited time. Research and practice has shown that not all cases require the same amount or type of supervision. In fact, it is possible to oversupervise cases and produce worse outcomes than

Assessing and understanding an offender's problems and needs is essential to formulating and carrying out an effective supervision strategy. *(Officer on the left.)*

would come with less supervision.

Setting priorities for supervision can be a formalized and systematic process based on statistical methods (see Chapter 3), or it can be left up to the individual officer to determine. In either case, probationers are assigned a priority level for their supervision, relative to the other cases in the caseload.

Decisions about case priority have implications beyond just the caseload officer. Some cases that are high priority in the eyes of the officers may or may not be those that the probation administrators or the judges think should be the priority.

One example of how this could be a problem: Probation officers make low-risk cases a priority, leaving the more difficult, high-risk cases with little supervision. They are oversupervising the low-risk cases, wasting their time and possibly producing worse outcomes by their involvement. In the meantime, the high-risk cases, which need close scrutiny and could benefit from supervision, are being neglected. An opportunity to produce better outcomes has been lost, and the likelihood that new crimes may have been committed is great. Research has shown that some high-risk offenders have a 50 percent or better chance of committing a new crime while under supervision (Petersilia et al. 1985; Administrative Office of the Courts 1991; Langan & Cunniff 1992).

To avoid this type of problem, probation supervisors should regularly review the priority decisions made by caseload officers. Formalized case management systems that emerged in probation across the country in the 1980s feature this kind of supervisory review. Even without formalized systems, some type of supervisor involvement is critical.

Supervision Planning

Once the probation officer has collected and analyzed the information about a case and has assigned a priority level, the next step is to develop a supervision strategy. This involves planning what the probationer will be expected to accomplish under supervision, what the probation officer will do to help, and what other resources will be involved. Much of this flows from the requirements of the court order, some from organizational policies, and the remainder from the probation officer's application of the general purposes of probation to the particular case.

It is important to keep in mind during the planning process that the primary focus of the supervision plan should be the probationer. The officer will assist, but the emphasis should be on the behavior of the probationer.

The way this planning function is handled varies widely. Some organizations have formalized and structured systems with elements such as written case plans, behavioral contracts, specific supervision strategies based on structured case assessments, and case conferences and staffings. In other organizations, there is far less structure, and officers handle case planning in their own way.

The case planning function benefits from some structure. Written case plans provide a ready reference for probation officers as to essential elements of the case and supervision strategy. This can be helpful with a large caseload and busy reporting sessions, when there is little time to recall the key elements of a case.

In a written case plan, the strategy is laid out concisely and can be reviewed quickly and efficiently. If a colleague of a probation officer has to cover in the event the officer is out of the office (in court, on vacation), a written case plan allows the colleague to step in and provide some continuity of supervision.

Case plans can also facilitate the supervision process. Probationers—whether because of a desire to manipulate the system or a genuine lack of recall—will often forget what they agreed to or were asked to do.

Once the supervision strategy has been developed, it becomes the road map for the supervision process.

Implementing the Strategy

Probation officers engage in a diverse range of activities to implement the supervision plan. The activities generally focus on one of the three major roles of probation: monitoring, enforcement, and services.

Monitoring

Monitoring is perhaps the most common activity and is basic to supervision because the other activities (enforcement and services) depend on knowing what the probationer is doing. Monitoring is done through office reports, where the probationer comes to the probation office or a satellite reporting station in the community. It is also accomplished through field visits, where the probation officer goes into the community for direct observation. Field visits may be made to the probationer's home, place of employment, or other places, such as training programs, counseling centers, or schools. Probation officers may contact others besides the probationer during field visits, including family members, neighbors, employers and co-workers, police officers, counselors, and anyone else who may be able to shed light on the activities of the probationer.

Increasingly, probation officers have technology to assist them in their monitoring. The two most common are urine testing for drug abuse and electronic surveillance to monitor the whereabouts of the probationer. (See Chapters 7 and 8.)

Enforcement

When monitoring indicates a probationer is not complying with the requirements of the court order or case plan, some efforts at enforcement are made. This can range from a discussion at the next reporting session about the importance of complying to filing violation-of-probation charges with the court. There are many steps in between these two strategies.

Services

In some instances, information gained through monitoring may indicate services are needed. This covers the full range of problems a probationer might have. It may be that a urine test turned up evidence of drug use, and thus enrollment in a treatment program would be called for. Loss of employment might suggest some type of training or vocational assessment is needed.

Probation officers act as brokers of services for probationers. By knowing about the types of services available, program requirements and costs, hours of service, eligibility guidelines, and other information about community-based agencies, officers can make referrals of probationers to services that can best address the problem at hand. Once a probationer engages the service, the probation officer then monitors the probationer's performance.

Keeping the Strategy Current

Everyone, including probationers, experiences change in his or her life. Some of these changes may affect their probation. As a result, the supervision strategy initially developed may be inappropriate in six months. Therefore, probation officers should update their supervision plans regularly.

It is important to regularly reassess and update the supervision strategy to keep it current to the needs and situation of the probationer. If change is not monitored and accommodated through reassessments, probationers who have made progress and who need less attention may be

oversupervised. On the other hand, probationers who have experienced a crisis and need more supervision may be undersupervised.

New Supervision Techniques

To learn more about which supervision strategies work with probationers, some researchers have begun to examine what occurs during the process of providing probation supervision. They have begun to develop programs based on strategies that have proven effective at improving outcomes.

Cognitive skills or life skills have been studied. Research has shown that many offenders have deficits in basic reasoning and coping skills needed to live in today's complex world (Ross & Fabiano 1985; Ross & Ross 1989). Without these skills such as problem solving, cognitive reasoning, interpersonal relations, and sensitivity to consequences, their decisions and responses to stressful or challenging situations are often inappropriate and may be illegal. Based on this, programs have been designed to remedy deficiencies in cognitive skills through a series of educational and experiential sessions. The initial findings from this approach are positive.

Another promising area is the development of programs designed to respond to the needs of a particular offender type or an offender who commits a particular type of offense. Examples of these are drug offender programs, where the underlying drug addiction produces criminality both in illegal drug dealing and other crimes committed to support the drug habit.

Offense-specific programs include those for drunk drivers, sex offenders, shoplifters, and domestic violence offenders. By targeting groups of offenders with similar characteristics or problems, interventions that have proven effective can be tailored to the needs of the group.

The supervision process is complex, dynamic, and challenging. It involves all of the probation officer's myriad assortment of skills, knowledge, and expertise. The task of managing the supervision process for one hundred or more probationers is a daunting one. Probation officers can draw on a number of tools and strategies that can help make the probation supervision process more manageable and more effective.

Violation of Probation

The primary goal of probation supervision is to ensure the offender complies with the requirements of the court order. The effective probation officer uses a variety of tools to gain compliance. However, as with almost any human endeavor, there are cases where compliance is not forthcoming.

Violation of probation is a formal charge brought by a probation officer against a probationer alleging that the probationer failed to comply with specific requirements of the court's sentence to probation.

Revocation is the termination of probation by the court for the offender's failure to comply with the conditions of the court's order. Revocation is based on the court finding the probationer guilty of the violation.

Monitoring probationers provides information to probation officers about their activities and levels of compliance. Once evidence of failure to comply emerges, a process of evaluating begins. Officers attempt to determine whether this is a willful failure to comply or whether there are circumstances that, while not excusing noncompliance, help to explain it.

In many jurisdictions, a new arrest or new conviction for a crime is a violation of probation. No determination of willfulness is required. In many instances, the judge will await the outcome of a new arrest before disposing of the violation-of-probation charge that is based on a new arrest.

Willful failure to comply, although a tough standard to reach, nonetheless can be proven. If a probationer is consciously and purposefully failing to abide by restrictions or comply with obligations, then there is a strong case for a judgment of willful failure. At this point, some action must be taken by the probation officer to notify the probationer that there is noncompliance and that some sanction may be imposed if behavior doesn't change.

When the officer determines there is no willful failure to comply but there still is noncompliance, a variety of strategies can be undertaken. If, for example, a urine test showed evidence of drug use, a probationer might be referred for drug evaluation or treatment. In the event of a failure to pay a fine or restitution order, the probation officer may review the probationer's financial situation. Perhaps a budget could be developed or the payment schedule adjusted to better fit the probationer's ability to pay.

Whatever the response, the probation officer attempts to gain compliance through working with the probationer, providing assistance, and using community resources and services to address problems that may be causing or contributing to noncompliance. It is not reasonable to expect perfection from probationers. Probation officers should

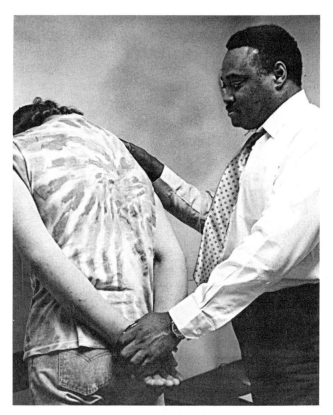

Failure to comply with court-ordered requirements of probation can lead to revocation. *(Officer on the right.)*

work with probationers, not just sanction them when they fail.

There are two types of probation violations commonly encountered. The first is a violation for new criminal activity, whether an arrest or a conviction. Violations based on new criminal activity are generally viewed as serious breaches of the court order. In many jurisdictions, new criminal activity, with or without a conviction, is sufficient to have the violation sustained and incarceration imposed.

The second type of violation of probation is the technical violation. Technical violations are based on failure to comply with the conditions of probation, rather than on new criminal activity. These violations are less clear cut and require substantial work on the part of the probation officer to prove willful failure. Technical violations can include noncompliance with both standard and special conditions of probation.

Once the decision to file violation-of-probation charges has been made, there is a series of steps that follow. Part of this process stems from cases decided by the U.S. Supreme Court, where questions of due process in the probation violation and revocation process are considered. In brief, the violation-of-probation process is not the same as the full criminal court process, but there are due process protections that must be provided the probationer. In general, the violation process is viewed not as a new criminal charge (leaving aside the new crime, if that is the basis for the violation), but rather it is a continuation of the original case for which the offender was placed on probation. When a new crime is involved, it is common for the violation-of-probation proceedings to be merged with the new crime for purposes of sentencing.

The probationer charged with a violation of probation has the following due process rights:

- the right to legal counsel

- the right to a notice of the alleged violations

- the right to appear and present evidence and witnesses and to confront adverse witnesses

- the right to a preliminary hearing to determine probable cause and a final, more comprehensive hearing dealing with revocation

Once the violation is before the court, a series of decisions has to be made. Probable cause must be determined by deciding whether there is sufficient evidence to proceed with the violation. If probable cause is found, then another hearing is held, addressing the guilt or innocence of the probationer. If the violation is sustained (a finding of guilty), then the court must determine the appropriate disposition.

In most jurisdictions, the court may impose any sentence on a violation of probation that could have been imposed at sentencing for the original crime. That provides a range of options, from continuing the probation, with or without changes to the term or conditions, to incarceration in jail or state prison. It is possible, although rather unusual, to dismiss probation altogether.

The court's disposition for a violation depends on many factors, including the seriousness of the violation, the probationer's situation, and plea negotiation, which occurs in the violation process as well as in sentencing. Another factor that enters into the disposition process is crowding of jails and prisons.

Accountability

The concept of accountability can be the key to a full understanding of the probation violation process. There is little disagreement that probationers must be held accountable for their actions: the crime for which they have been convicted and sentenced and the court's terms for probation.

Accountability is also a key issue for probation officers, who are held accountable by their supervisors for complying with the policies and procedures of the probation organization. They are also held accountable by the judges, whose orders they are carrying out.

Just as probation supervisors and administrators hold caseload officers accountable, so too should they be held accountable. This means having clear and effective policies and procedures; having appropriate levels of resources, whether staff or otherwise; providing timely and appropriate training; and giving adequate supervision to caseload officers.

Accountability is also an issue for judges in the violation process. Probation organizations rely on judges' support when charging probationers with violations. When violations are dismissed, or if they are sustained, and the probationer is continued on probation without any real sanction, officers who have reached the decision that some sanction is needed are undermined. Probationers get the impression that noncompliance really has no consequences. The authority of the probation officer is seriously eroded. The integrity of the court's order is also compromised when probationers fail to obey the order and are not sanctioned or punished for that failure.

When viewed in this way, accountability becomes a concern for all involved, from the probationer to the judge. Effective probation supervision can be achieved only when all parties are accountable for their responsibilities.

Enforcement Techniques

One of the problems facing probation officers and judges as they deal with violations of probation is the lack of options to use in sentencing. Judges can impose any sanction at violation that could have been imposed originally. The problem is that there are not many options available.

There is little a judge can do to sanction a violator short of incarceration. Incarceration is a costly response and one that represents the ultimate authority of the court. In many jurisdictions, intermediate options do not exist, and the choice is jail or continuing probation. Judges become frustrated because jail is too strong a response, but there is nothing else. Probation officers become frustrated because they get the same offenders back again and again. Officers may begin to hold back on violations they should file because they become cynical about the probability of any meaningful outcome. Probationers get the wrong message: that they can violate the conditions of probation with impunity.

To address this problem, many jurisdictions are experimenting with intermediate sanctions (see Chapter 6). These are programs or sentencing options that fall between probation and prison. They provide a greater array of choices for judges to choose from in punishing probation violators. With such options, it is more likely that a judge would find a sanction that has some punitive value but does not require invoking the full measure of punishment that incarceration represents. If judges had these options and made regular use of them, probation officers would be less likely to resist filing necessary violation charges based on an expectation of no action being taken. The message would ultimately get to the probationer that there are consequences that come with failure to comply with the court's order.

In addition to increasing sentencing options, many jurisdictions are experimenting with alternatives to the traditional violation-of-probation process. These include using hearing officers or supervisory level probation staff to hold administrative hearings. These take place prior to a case being returned to court and are designed to let the probationer know in a formal way that noncompliance is a problem and that some sanction will be imposed. In these hearings, an attempt is often made to modify the court order or enter into some type of agreement to gain compliance.

Other techniques in this area include special judges and enforcement days where the entire court calendar is devoted to enforcement cases. In the area of financial obligations like restitution and fines, some probation agencies are pursuing wage garnishments and civil judgments to collect overdue obligations.

Effectiveness of Sanctions

A full range of intermediate sanctions would facilitate the development and implementation of a more effective system of sanctioning violations of probation. The following three principles underlie an effective sanctioning system:

1. Timeliness. To be meaningful, a sanction must be imposed in a timely manner, close in time to the behavior being sanctioned. The officer should file the charges promptly, and the court should dispose of the violation promptly. The more time that elapses, the less effective the sanction will be.

2. Certainty. There must be a degree of certainty to any sanctioning system. If there is not a high probability that a sanction will result from prohibited behavior, there is little deterrent value in the prohibition. Probationers must know that they are likely to be punished if they do not comply.

3. Measured, incremental responses. If the first two principles are observed, then it will not be necessary to invoke the serious sanction of incarceration as frequently. More measured responses will achieve the goals if they are timely and certain. It is when sanctions are far removed in time from the violation and so uncertain that harsh sanctions like incarceration become necessary to get the probationer's attention. By then, it is probably too late.

Evaluating the Effectiveness of Probation Supervision

The field of evaluation is large and complex, one that can be daunting. It is not necessary to get into sophisticated design methodologies and statistical calculations to begin to address the questions of "how well are we doing?" and "what effect are we having?"

Traditionally, probation and other correctional programs have been evaluated on recidivism, the rate at which probationers get reinvolved in criminal activity. Although recidivism is a popular measure of effectiveness, it has some serious limitations.

Using Recidivism as a Measure

The first thing to do when using recidivism as a measure of program success is to determine the criteria. What qualifies an offender as a recidivist? Is it a new arrest? A new conviction? A conviction for a similar crime? Or a more serious crime? What about a lesser crime?

If the probationer is not convicted, does that count? If incarceration is not imposed, is that recidivism? What is the timeframe for monitoring the probationer's behavior? Is it only while the probationer is under supervision? Is there a follow-up period, after discharge from probation? How long is that period?

The answers to these questions will produce different definitions of recidivism. These definitions, applied to the same population of offenders, will produce different recidivism rates. The difference in rates for the same population can often be twenty percentage points or more. Differences that great can cast a probation organization or program in very different lights, some of which are much less positive.

Until a standardized definition of recidivism is accepted, this fundamental problem will persist. A standard definition was proposed in the 1970s by the National Commission on Criminal Justice Standards and Goals, but it has not been widely embraced. Each researcher or evaluator develops his or her own definition, based on funding limits, availability of records, and political considerations. As recidivism definitions proliferate, it becomes harder to compare programs with one another. The search for effective program models becomes more difficult.

A similar problem exists with technical violations of probation—ones that result from enforcement activities of probation officers. If monitoring reveals noncompliance or inappropriate behavior and the probationer is returned to jail by the judge on a violation of probation, how should that case be counted? Is it a failure because probation was revoked and the offender returned to jail? Or, should it be viewed as a success because the officer detected the noncompliant behavior and took the offender off the street?

There are also some basic difficulties with using recidivism as the sole or primary measure of probation effectiveness. When new criminal activity is measured, the focus is on the offender's behavior. Although controlling criminal activity is a legitimate goal of probation, the technology and methods used do not effectively reduce criminal behavior. With an average caseload nationally of well above 100, in some places upwards of 300, probation officers have perhaps ten minutes per week to devote to a case (Criminal Justice Institute 1993). That includes all activities on a case, not just personal contact.

Under these circumstances, it is unrealistic to expect probation officers to routinely deter new criminal activity. Even under the best circumstances, where caseloads are under fifty, probationers still spend a majority of their time away from the officer and under many negative influences.

It is difficult to justify using recidivism as the sole measure of effectiveness when it focuses on something outside the probation officer's control. Some measure of new criminal activity should be used, but it needs to be combined with other realistic and appropriate measures.

New and Better Measures

Measures of the probation supervision process should examine both the ultimate effectiveness of supervision (the outcome) and how well the process itself is being carried out (the performance level). In this way, there will be several measures on which to assess probation.

First, to be considered is how well is the job being done? Are probation officers complying with all the policies and procedures that govern supervision? Is the process of supervision being faithfully carried out? Are priority levels being established and implemented? Are supervision plans being developed and followed? These are things for which officers can directly and fairly be held accountable. These are the things more or less under the control of the probation officer.

The next thing to examine is what does this process produce? What are the outcomes of applying this process to these probationers? The most common time to do outcome assessments is at the end of the supervision term. Statements about money collected, hours of community service performed, drug test results, and criminal activity are the kinds of specific outcome measures to consider when closing the case. Outcome measures should also be made at various points in time during supervision to provide interim measures and assessment of progress.

When these types of outcome and performance measures are combined with recidivism measures, a more accurate picture of probation supervision emerges. This comprehensive approach allows one to draw reliable conclusions about what works. Knowing the performance level on policy implementation makes it easier to conclude that a given program approach or process does or does not work. Much of the recent literature evaluating intensive supervision programs show equal results when compared with regular probation (Petersilia & Turner 1990, 1993; U.S. GAO 1993a, 1993b, 1993c). In many of those studies, the program did not meet the requirements for supervision set forth in its model. So rather than stating that the intensive supervision model did not work, all that can be said is that the model was not implemented as it was designed.

This multipart measurement model places responsibilities where they belong. Probation officers are accountable for carrying out the policies and procedures of their organization. Administrators and managers are accountable for seeing that officers have the training and resources to comply with procedures. Recidivism is still used as a measure, but it is part of a more balanced approach.

Conclusion

The supervision of probationers is an important, but one of the least understood, functions of the juvenile and criminal justice systems. Probation is the disposition most often used in criminal and juvenile courts. Almost four times as many people are on probation as are in custody (Bureau of Justice Statistics 1992).

Yet, probation continues to labor in obscurity, despite the fact that almost all probationers live in the community. They aren't visible because they are dispersed throughout cities and towns. Probationers aren't collected in one place, like inmates. Thus, caseload crowding tends not to be noticed except by probation agencies.

Effective supervision of probationers can help prevent crime in communities, making them better places to live. It can also help keep probationers working; thereby allowing them to support dependents and pay taxes. By referring probationers with problems to community services or programs, probation can reduce the likelihood of offenders facing more difficulties and the potential for future crimes.

Probation as currently practiced is less expensive, by a wide margin, than incarceration. Even the most expensive probation programs (like intensive supervision) are one-fourth the cost of incarceration (Administrative Office of the Courts 1993). When other benefits, such as employment-related contributions, collection of fines and restitution, and community service, are added, the cost-benefit analysis tips even further toward probation. Perhaps the most compelling argument for probation is that if it is effective and keeps a probationer out of the criminal justice system in the future, the costs of that person's future criminal justice involvement can be avoided. It is here that the greatest potential for probation supervision can be found.

References

Administrative Office of the Courts. 1991. *Bergen Probation Division risk assessment research project final report.* Trenton, N.J.: Administrative Office of the Courts.

Administrative Office of the Courts. 1993. *New Jersey Intensive Supervision Program Progress Report* 10 (1).

Bureau of Justice Statistics. 1992. *National Update* 1 (3).

Criminal Justice Institute. 1993. *The corrections yearbook.* South Salem, N.Y.: Criminal Justice Institute.

Langan, P. A., and M. A. Cunniff. 1992. *Recidivism of felons on probation.* Washington, D.C.: U.S. Department of Justice, Bureau of Justice Statistics.

Petersilia, J., and S. Turner. 1990. *Intensive supervision for high risk probationers.* Santa Monica, Calif.: Rand Corporation

———. 1993. *Evaluating intensive supervision probation/parole: Results of a national experiment.* Washington, D.C.: National Institute of Justice.

Petersilia, J., et al. 1985. *Granting felons probation.* Santa Monica, Calif.: Rand Corporation.

Ross, R. R., and E. Fabriano. 1985. *Time to think: A cognitive model of delinquency prevention and offender rehabilitation.* Johnson City, Tenn.: Institute of Social Sciences and Arts.

Ross, R. R., and B. D. Ross. 1989. Delinquency prevention through cognitive training. *Education Horizons* (Summer).

U.S. General Accounting Office. 1993a. Intensive probation supervision: *Mixed effectiveness in controlling crime.* Washington, D.C.: U.S. GAO.

U.S. General Accounting Office. 1993b. *Intensive probation supervision: Cost savings relative to incarceration.* Washington, D.C.: U.S. GAO.

U.S. General Accounting Office. 1993c. *Intensive probation supervision: Crime control and cost-saving effectiveness.* Washington, D.C.: U.S. GAO.

APPLICABLE ACA STANDARDS

Standards for Adult Probation and Parole Field Services
Management Information and Research 2-3096
Supervision—Probation and Parole Agencies 2-3103 to 2-3105, 2-3106, 2-3108, 2-3109, 2-3111, 2-3114, 2-3116, 2-3120, 2-3127, 2-3129 to 2-3132, 2-3136, 2-3145
Supervision—Probation Agencies Only 2-3184

5

Supervision of Parolees

By Edward J. Dolan

Parole supervision has been around in one form or another for more than one hundred years. Many strategies and technologies used in parole supervision evolved in response to an increase in violent parolees, to higher numbers of parolees, and to the continuing mandate to protect the public.

Parole supervision varies from one state to another. Differences in agency locus, authority, responsibilities, organization, and resources affect the intensity and effectiveness of supervision.

Some states combine discretionary release, the parole board, and supervision in one agency. A number of jurisdictions have joined parole and probation agencies, other states place community supervision within corrections departments, and a few states have abolished parole. Virtually all states retain both discretionary release as well as supervision functions in some form.

Whether it is called "parole," "community corrections," or "community reintegration," it is generally recognized that a gradual release to the community of incarcerated offenders is preferable to out-right release from a public safety, social service, and cost perspective. Some degree of postincarceration supervision should occur in the community if a correctional system is to maintain a process of graduated release.

Release to the community is conditional in virtually all jurisdictions. That is, certain behaviors are required of the offender and certain behaviors are prohibited. Supervision

---

Edward J. Dolan is executive director of the Massachusetts Parole Board.

entails both enforcement and support of these behavioral conditions by the offender in a community setting.

The tools of parole supervision vary by jurisdiction and by case. Successful officers employ both law enforcement and social service strategies, techniques, and technologies to manage offenders in the community.

Effective case management begins with identifying aspects of offenders' daily lives that are associated with their past criminal behavior and, therefore, their future compliance or noncompliance with the conditions of release. This identification process and the setting of release conditions is most often done by a discretionary release authority.

A second element of effective supervision is the supervision strategy or case plan. This strategy or plan lays out the goals for both the offender and the officer for the period of community supervision. The plan sets forth activities by which goals are to be achieved by the officer and offender. The plan also establishes milestones in terms of time and/or behavior against which progress can be measured.

Supervising offenders in the community involves routine, direct, and indirect monitoring of their behavior. This may mean monitoring an offender's routine itinerary, including employment/training, treatment, and home and leisure activities. Supervision includes direct contact with offenders to verify their behavior and monitor their attitudinal, physical, mental, and emotional condition. Effective supervision very often requires collateral contacts, which may include officer contact with the offender's family, counselors, treatment providers, employers, neighbors, and friends as a means of monitoring the offender's behavior. Other elements of supervision may include surveillance, electronic monitoring, supportive social services in the areas of housing, income maintenance, employment, training and education, mandated substance abuse and mental or physical health treatment, and substance abuse testing.

In view of all of this, it remains that the crux of parole supervision is a parole officer's contact with parolees in the community. Parole officers are the agents by which supervision occurs. They enforce laws and parole conditions. Their duties are ideally balanced between public safety and social services. This balance hinges on parolee behavior, agency priorities, and the officer's training, experience, and attitudes. It is also affected by public and media perceptions about certain crimes and populations.

Agency Mission and Supervisory Authority

Each government entity charged with parole supervision should have a mission statement to guide its staff in meeting the goals of the agency. The mission statement may be shaped by statutes, executive orders, policies and procedures, and public perception. All facets of the parole agency should be focused on the mission so that services are delivered expediently and effectively.

Although the mission statement is not necessarily static, the basic premise of parole supervision—that is, community contact with the parolee—should remain the same.

The extent of the agency's and its officers' authority is generally set by statutes. Parole is an executive function, whereas probation generally is a judicial function. It is sometimes further regulated by its placement within corrections or probation departments.

Case Assignments

Inmates who receive a parole release date are assigned to a parole officer. Assignments to an officer may be made on the basis of residence and geographical districts, specialized caseloads, and workload formulas.

Caseloads may be virtually limitless in number, or they may be restricted as to the number of parolees assigned to each officer.

Initial Interview

The paroling authority sets conditions of release. The conditions, at least initially, define the supervision plan formulated by the officer. There are general conditions of parole that all parolees must abide by and then there are special conditions of parole individually tailored to address specific problems and needs of parolees.

In conjunction with formulating the supervision plan, the parole officer is responsible for classifying the parolee into a level of supervision. Levels of supervision dictate the minimal standards of contact that a parole officer must meet on each case. For example, some agencies use a classification instrument called Risks/Needs Assessment; after completion of the instrument a risk score and a needs score is computed. The scores are compared to a matrix and the outcome is a specific level of supervision.

Generally, the parole officer conducts an initial interview with the parolee. The parole officer prepares for this interview by reviewing the case folder, which includes not only parole-generated material, but information gathered by institutional parole staff from police, courts, district attorney's office, probation, social service and treatment agencies, family, friends, and the parolee. The initial interview is the prime opportunity for the parole officer to gather as much information from the parolee as possible about the parolee's family, friends, hangouts, and so forth. It is also the time to set the tone of the relationship. The parole officer should be friendly, but not a friend. Officers should make it clear to parolees that certain things are required and the officers are there to enforce them. Parole officers are also there to keep parolees in the community by helping them with their problems.

During the interview, which can take place at the parole office or at the parolee's residence, the parole officer reviews the parole conditions, ensuring the parolee's and the parole officer's copies of the parole release papers are the same. The parole officer then orients the parolee as to what the parole conditions mean, explains what is expected of the parolee, and discusses the possible consequences for violating parole conditions. The parole officer should never tell the parolee that a certain action will be taken before it occurs, especially if the parole officer does not have the authority to back up the statement.

The officer then reviews the level of supervision, standards of contact, and overall supervision plan with the parolee. Depending on the jurisdiction, the parole officer may give the parolee a copy of the parolee grievance procedure. The parole officer may take this opportunity to have the parolee make contacts with others who have an interest in the parolee (e.g., probation officers, courts, substance abuse treatment vendors), as well as to determine if the parolee has a driver's license and vehicle.

Finally, the officer should inform the parolee of the parole officer's supervisor's name, office schedule, and business and emergency phone numbers. The next contact is then scheduled.

Relationship between Parole Officers and Parolees

Parole officers are law enforcement and social services agents. They continually strive to maintain the delicate balance between the two responsibilities. There are some guiding principles that officers should follow during the course of supervising parolees.

Officers must comply with certain codes of conduct that govern their relationships with parolees. Officers represent the state and as such have a public trust. They must be aware of any possible violations of this trust, intentional or not, that could jeopardize their position and good name. Their relationships with parolees should not involve any business or commercial dealings, they should not condone violations of parole or illegalities, they should avoid conflict-of-interest situations, they must avoid romantic or friendship involvements, and they should not use threats or coercion or be involved in collusion of any type.

Officers should attempt to treat all parolees by the same standards, expectations, and sanctions. They should be mindful of casework principles and treat parolees as human beings who have the needs, wants, and desires of anyone else, albeit with less expectations of privacy and freedom because of their parole status. Parolees may need to vent their feelings, and parole officers have to decide if it is positive behavior or behavior that could lead to additional problems.

Parole officers deal with many different personalities, from antisocial types to manic-depressives to psychopaths.

They must deal with different sexes, sexual lifestyles, races, ethnic groups, and religions. It is difficult to know about and understand all of these groups and at the same time impose more or less the same standards and conditions on them and expect the same response. It is also difficult for parole officers not to make value judgments based on each individual officer's norms, mores, attitudes, and upbringing. There are also areas in a parolee's life that are sensitive (e.g., sexual and marital relationships) that parole officers have to learn how to deal with and discuss with the parolee.

The manner in which parole officers conduct themselves with parolees sets the tone for supervision. It will dictate how a parolee responds to a parole officer's instructions and overall supervision. Parolees for all their bravado and manipulatory behavior are generally apprehensive about being on parole. They see the parole officer as the person who can send them back to jail. Parole officers should try to foster a trusting relationship with parolees and not use their authority and badge as a means to threaten or intimidate parolees. Parole officers can understand and accept the problems of a parolee without compromising their authority.

The manner in which officers conduct themselves with offenders sets the tone for supervision. *(Officer on the left.)*

Supervision in the Community

For the most part, parole officers work alone in the community. They must be familiar with the area in which they work, not only in terms of geography, but in terms of social service resources, local politics and issues, law enforcement and criminal justice assistance, community problems, and so forth.

Once officers are familiar with their area in general, they must acquaint themselves with the neighborhoods where the parolees reside. Certain areas should be approached with caution (e.g., with another parole officer or at certain times of the day).

Parole officers should be aware that they represent the state, and how they conduct themselves in the community is important. Officers set examples for parolees. They are professionals and should act accordingly. Their work in the community should be discreet, and they should respect the confidentiality of the parolee's status and the privacy rights of the home sponsors and employers.

When visiting offenders at their place of employment, officers should be discreet and respect the confidentiality of the offenders' status. (*Officer on the left.*)

A parole officer's approach to the job is developed from training, experience, and common sense. There will be situations for which officers cannot be totally prepared, and many officers may not handle them well. But officers should not avoid these situations; they should do the best they can and learn from them. Parole officers should not be reluctant to contact their supervisors or fellow officers for advice and help.

If possible, parole officers should make unannounced visits to parolees' homes at reasonable hours. The purpose of home visits is to observe the parolee and the residence, ensure compliance with parole conditions, address problems and crises in the parolee's life, control risk, take urine specimens, and gather and update information regarding the parolee's adjustment.

Parole officers should prepare themselves for home visits or contacts in the community. They should carry authorized, issued equipment (e.g., firearm, restraints, a chemical agent, vest, two-way radio, etc.). They should review the parolee's records and conditions to prepare questions for the interview. They should prepare themselves mentally for crisis situations that may occur (e.g., domestic violence, child abuse, or an attack on the officer). Many officers receive training on nonviolent crisis intervention and/or escalation/de-escalation techniques. Finally, they should be knowledgeable of agency policies and procedures that pertain to the officers' powers, responsibilities, and liabilities.

During the investigation of the parolee's home program, parole officers have the opportunity to initiate a relationship with the home sponsor. The home sponsor can be an important information resource for the parole officer especially when a parolee is beginning to exhibit signs of substance abuse, keeping late hours, hanging out with the wrong people, missing work, and other instances that indicate regression.

Parole officers are also responsible for documenting their work on each parolee in various reports, chronological records, daily notebooks/diaries, and logs. Documentation of all visits, contacts, phone conversations, investigations, and even no contacts is vital to supervision and case management. Documentation and report writing are also crucial in the parole violation process from preliminary hearings to final revocation hearings.

These records provide accountability controls for supervisors and management and documentation for courts in response to subpoenas, liability issues, and lawsuits.

Supervision Strategies

Parole officers are often left to their own devices and creativity to supervise parolees, and these are developed over time with experience. But there are many things parole officers should do to enhance their ability to supervise parolees.

Parole officers should be familiar with all the resources in the area they cover, including criminal justice agencies and social service agencies. They should be aware of the different neighborhoods in the communities they are assigned to cover. Personal contacts with these agencies can make it easier for officers to obtain records, make referrals, obtain detoxification beds, and so forth.

Routine contact with local police is important in terms of good professional working relationships and assistance in supervision, surveillance, and apprehension. The police can act as a supplement to supervision by providing parole officers with verbal and written reports about parolees. These reports can range from casual, informal discussions to field observation reports to arrest reports.

Parole officers should maintain contact with substance abuse and mental health providers. The information exchanged can range from attendance records to valuable insight into a parolee's behavior and intentions. Many times this information can help parole officers actively prevent technical and substantive violations.

Contact with the parolee's employment, school, or training center is beneficial in monitoring compliance with conditions and determining if a parolee actually intends to help himself or herself. It is not always sufficient just to check pay stubs to verify work; it may be necessary to observe a parolee going to or leaving from work. The parole officer, however, should not do anything that would jeopardize the parolee's employment or participation in programs. It is also helpful to stop by the parolee's home during times the parolee is supposed to be at work or in school. The officer should not assume that the parolee is in fact at these places.

Collateral contacts with probation officers in the cases of dual supervision can be beneficial by sharing information and supervision strategies. It can also prevent the parolee from playing one officer against another officer.

Parole officers may also obtain information about a parolee just by driving by certain streets and areas of the district at different times and days of the week.

Supplements to Supervision

Supplements to supervision are developed routinely; however, because of funding concerns, they are not at the disposal of all agencies. These strategies can assist the officer during supervision, but they should not be used as substitutes for in-person parolee and parole officer contacts. These strategies can also be used as sanctions for relatively minor parole violations.

Halfway houses are particularly helpful to parole officers in that they have a variety of uses. The function of most halfway houses is to treat alcohol and drug abusers. However, in some jurisdictions, halfway houses are used in release programs for inmates, as temporary residences for parolees on the street, or as halfway back sanctions for parolees experiencing difficulties meeting parole conditions.

Some agencies use electronic monitoring devices worn by parolees. A parole officer is still required to make parolee in-person contacts and to respond to negative reports generated by the device. Many times electronic monitoring is used as an initial release strategy for certain inmates (e.g., those serving time for driving under the influence), and it can also be used as a sanction for technical parole violations or in conjunction with house detention.

Urine testing is an important element in supervision of most offenders because many have experienced substance abuse problems. Officers can be trained to use testing apparatuses that are easy to use in the office or in the field. Generally, officers use instruments that serve as a screening test, and if the tests are positive, they are then sent to a laboratory for confirmation. The screening tests can give instant results and therefore enable the officer to impose immediate sanctions.

A few jurisdictions are trying innovative programs to deal with specific populations. For example, intensive parole programs are used to supervise high-risk offenders who require a high frequency of contacts, testing, and surveillance. Most of these programs require officers to work in teams in specific areas of the cities.

Another program being considered by some agencies is specifically geared to sex offenders. These offenders are often treated like any other offender and do not receive the attention they require because they are not generally like the typical offender. In this program, the parole officer is the case manager of a team that includes parole officers for supervision and surveillance, a polygraph examiner for random testing and information on a parolee's activities, and a qualified clinician who conducts group therapy sessions. This team meets regularly to share information that can be used to keep the sex offender from reoffending.

Programs for female parolees have been gaining more support. The female population faces a variety of obstacles that prevent it from obtaining the necessary assistance in the community that it needs to remain on the street. Homes for pregnant parolees, employment and training programs, battered women's shelters, and multifaceted programs that address child care issues, self-esteem, prenatal care, health issues, and substance abuse issues are being proposed and funded in many states.

Some agencies have officers specifically trained to supervise developmentally disabled and mentally retarded parolees. This population is extremely difficult to work with because these parolees demand a lot of attention. With the proper resources, this type of program can be successful in dealing with parolees regular parole officers do not have sufficient time and training to supervise.

More and more agencies are also realizing the value of criminal justice and law enforcement computer programs. With these computer programs, agencies can access statewide networks to obtain information on criminal records, outstanding warrants, and driver's licenses. In some states it is possible to access statewide court, probation, and corrections information. There are also networks that provide communication capabilities necessary to exchange information on parolees, regardless of their location.

Many other strategies are being developed and tested, but the essence of parole supervision is face-to-face contact with the parolee and others in the community.

Parole Violations

Parole officers are generally law enforcement officers as defined in each particular state. They are sworn in as peace officers, deputy sheriffs, or special state police of-

ficers. They are authorized to investigate and report on parole violations and, if necessary, arrest parole violators.

To effect parole warrants, many officers are trained in the use of restraints, arrest procedures, transportation of inmates, search and seizure, report writing, use of chemical agents, and use of firearms. Parole officers may arrest parole violators with the assistance of other parole officers or depend primarily on local and state police for assistance.

Parole violations may be minor or major. A minor violation is misconduct that is of a less serious nature and does not involve a threat to public safety or the safety of the parolee. Minor violations may be addressed by the parole officer through verbal warnings together with a

In light of an offender's violation of parole requirements, the officer may seek a warrant for the offender's arrest.

concrete strategy to deal with the specific problem (e.g., in the first instance of substance abuse, the parolee must attend counseling and submit to random urinalysis). These violations can also be addressed through case conferences with the supervisor, the parole officer, and the parolee. The case conference is used to identify issues, address specific problems, gauge the seriousness of infractions, and impose sanctions that do not require parole board action. The supervisor should also address the issues with concrete action so that the parolee knows that continued misconduct will be dealt with more severely.

Major violations generally involve violent acts against a person, acts showing a lack of impulse control, serious property offenses, or repeated technical violations of parole conditions. These violations involve the safety of the community and/or the parolee (e.g., new arrest for a felony, child abuse, or domestic violence).

Parole officers must investigate all violations of parole conditions within certain time frames and submit a report to their supervisor. The seriousness of the violations, the threat to public safety, the likelihood an offender will flee, and the potential for more serious behavior will determine whether the parolee is detained pending a hearing to address the violations. *Morrissey v. Brewer* determined that parolees must be given certain rights of a hearing on the alleged violations, notification of the alleged violations, the time and place of the hearing, and other rights concerning counsel and the right to speak or say nothing.

The parole officer must determine the parole conditions violated, investigate each one promptly, obtain documentation (e.g., police report and court records) to support the violations, arrange for the parolee's hearing, submit a written report on the parole violations, and in some jurisdictions, attend the revocation hearing.

Parole officers should use a method of graduated sanctions if possible to handle parole violations. The primary goals to keep in mind are public safety and helping the parolee remain in the community. The first option for violations, especially technical violations, should not be detention and revocation.

Parole officers must be firm, fair, and consistent in addressing parole violations. Parolees must have an understanding of what they did and why it is a violation. Parole officers must be careful to enforce parole conditions uniformly because parolees communicate with one another and share information about what parole officers do or don't do.

Parole officers should not be reluctant to recommend that a parolee be detained. They should be sensitive to the loss of liberty issue and not take it lightly, but if the parolee is a danger to himself or herself or others, then the proper action is detention. The public, victims, and potential victims demand that parole officers protect the community.

Conclusion

The changing nature of offenders in the criminal justice system and extreme crowding in corrections facilities have added to the demands placed on paroling authorities. Effective supervision of the parolee in the community involves several elements, including identifying aspects of the offenders' lives that are linked with their past criminal behavior and their success on parole, developing a comprehensive supervision strategy or case plan, and following through with the plan.

Parole officers are continually faced with balancing their roles of law enforcement and social services. Their tasks are often difficult and involve being flexible and creative. The supervision of parolees is important to successfully reintegrating the offender into the community and ensuring public safety.

APPLICABLE ACA STANDARDS
Standards for Adult Probation and Parole Field Services
   Administration, Organization, and Management 2-3002, 2-3010, 2-3011
   Personnel 2-3050, 2-3051
   Training and Staff Development 2-3071
   Supervision—Probation and Parole Agencies 2-3105-1, 2-3105-2, 2-3106, 2-3110, 2-3111, 2-3114, 2-3129 to 2-3132, 2-3137 to 2-3141, 2-3146, 2-3149, 2-3162, 2-3163
   Supervision—Parole Agencies Only 2-3167 to 2-3169, 2-3172, 2-3173

6

Intermediate Sanctions and Probation

By Dennis R. Martin and Harvey M. Goldstein

Largely as a result of crowded prisons and jails, probation has become the sentencing option of choice. Nationally in 1990, five times as many convicted offenders were sentenced to probation (1,637,557) as were sentenced to state and federal institutions (323,069) (Bureau of Justice Statistics 1991). Although the number of probationers grew 234 percent from 1,137,529 in 1981 to 2,670,234 in 1991, expanding probation caseloads were not met with a concomitant growth in funding and resources (Bureau of Justice Statistics 1983, 1991). Consequently, the time available for each case dwindled to minutes per month, allowing little opportunity for effective intervention.

Another result of institutional crowding was the changing nature of the probation caseload. As jails and prisons filled to capacity, offenders who would previously have been incarcerated—those with extensive criminal records and those who have been convicted of serious offenses—found their way to probation supervision.

The original dynamics of probation have buckled under the weight of heavy caseloads. When John Augustus first started the practice in the mid-1800s, probation was voluntary, caseloads were small, and the emphasis was on individual attention. Close contact between officer and of-

fender was supposed to lead to a relationship that would influence the probationer to a more positive lifestyle. Individual attention would allow for problems to be diagnosed and a variety of approaches brought to bear to bring about behavioral change.

In response to heavy caseloads, probation agencies began case management through objective risk and needs assessment. By measuring and evaluating the probationer's problem areas (e.g., education, employment, substance abuse, and mental health) and the likelihood of the offender breaking the law again, cases could be ranked in terms of the effort needed from the officer. This approach offered a rational way to apportion staff time and other resources, but the problems caused by growing demands for service from a static resource pool persisted.

Corrections administrators, judges, and legislators sought to find additional approaches to managing offenders. They began to develop the concept of a continuum of graduated sanctions. This entailed sentencing options that fit between incarceration and probation while still emphasizing deterrence, punishment, restitution, and rehabilitation. These intermediate sanctions had to be credible, mete out punishment commensurate with the crime, provide close monitoring of offender behavior, and foster behavior change through service delivery.

The creativity and inventiveness of the states led to the development of a plethora of sanctions—some stand-alone options and others that could be added to prison or probation terms.

Dennis R. Martin works for the Probation Services Division of the New Jersey Administrative Office of the Courts.

Harvey M. Goldstein, president of the American Probation and Parole Association, is the assistant director for Probation in the New Jersey Administrative Office of the Courts.

Community Service

The concept of community service is based on the principle that crimes are detrimental to the community, not just to the individual victim. Therefore, it is fitting for the offender to repay the community through labor directed to the public good. In many situations, community service is mandated by statutes on conviction for a specific offense. The law may prescribe the number of hours required or allow the judge to set the length of time for community service within a certain range. Community service may also be used as an enhancement to a sentence that results from the violation of a prior sentence. In these instances, community service is added to the conditions imposed previously as part of a probation sentence or as part of conditions for parole from incarceration.

Because this involves giving back to the community—for the good of the public—community service is almost always performed on behalf of public agencies or nonprofit organizations. On rare occasions, defendants may be ordered to work for the victims of their crime or for needy individuals. However, these kinds of arrangements require special care and consideration to ensure the safety of the recipient. Community service is not usually rendered to profit-making corporations, unless it is a matter of direct restitution to the crime victim.

Many probation and parole departments supervise their own community service programs. Others contract out to social service agencies to do the administrative work. Community sites are identified, goals and objectives to be accomplished by the participants are determined, and job descriptions are drawn up. Probation and/or parole officials may supervise the work in progress, but frequently that task is left to the organization where the work is being done. Hours worked, failure to report, or any other problems are reported back to the supervising agency for intervention.

Although community service might be done by individuals working alone, under the guidance of host site personnel, more and more jurisdictions that successfully use community service are engaged in group work sites. In this situation, clusters of community service workers engage in a joint effort in a project. These groups of offenders may be seen in parks or along highways picking up trash or pulling weeds. Some judges have used these situations creatively for offenders who have not met other obligations under the original terms of community supervision (e.g., paying their restitution or attending drug treatment sessions). In one program, offenders were required to report daily for community service assignments until they had obtained regular employment. Part of the time, these individuals were being trained in job seeking skills.

Financial Sanctions

Courts have a long history of imposing monetary obligations on offenders as a means of punishment and as a way to recoup losses that resulted from the commission of the crime. Some financial sanctions are mandatory. That is, they must be imposed by the court either on all offenders or else on those who meet specific criteria, such as conviction for particular offenses, number of prior guilty verdicts, losses sustained by victims, and so forth. Other fines and fees are discretionary. Judges may impose such a fine as a means to enhance punishment, deter future criminal activity, and make recompense to the victim.

Funds collected from fines, fees, and assessments are used for a variety of purposes, including the following:

- restitution paid directly to individuals or organizations

- general restitution paid to victim compensation organizations

- funding for special programs, such as crime prevention initiatives

- fees for services, such as drug use monitoring or supervision

- general fund income for municipality, county, or state treasuries

- cost of the operation of the courts

The general theory underlying financial sanctions might be that they will provide general or specific deterrence, but they still serve a function even if those goals are not achieved. Specifically, the funds generated from these assessments are used for worthwhile purposes that benefit the community at large as well as individuals victimized by crime.

As with the types of financial penalties that may or must be assessed, the amounts are established by statute (depending on such factors as the nature and/or severity of the crime), fall within a prescribed range, or may be left entirely to the discretion of the judge. In the latter situation, the court may act on whim, preference, or tradition or may take into account the financial condition of the defendant. Income, debts, and outstanding liabilities may be

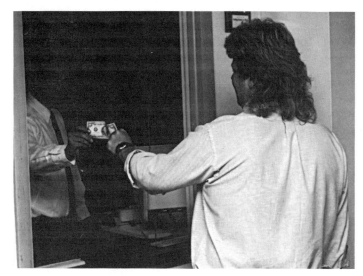

Fines or restitution are often included in the offender's probation or parole requirements.

considered when arriving at the amounts to be paid. When this is done, an increased emphasis may be placed on the punitive aspect of the sanction. That is to say, the defendant is being deprived of something very important in the form of financial gain being limited by the court. The so-called "day fine" system ranks all offenses by seriousness and assigns day-fine units as the penalty for being convicted of committing one of these crimes. The value of the day-fine unit is tied to the income of the offender. Therefore, if two people are convicted of the same action, and if one defendant is earning twice as much as a co-defendant, the one earning more will pay twice as much as the convicted defendant with the lower wages.

Collection of court-imposed monetary obligations is important to the operations of many programs, some of which are run by probation and the courts and others that operate under the auspices of other agencies. Consequently, community supervision programs are taking active steps to improve collection rates. A variety of methods are being used, including the following:

- wage attachments

- withholding of income tax refunds

- docketing of civil judgments as liens against real property

- seizure of property

- forfeiture of lottery or gambling winnings

Payments are being accepted by electronic funds transfer and credit card. With some telephone reporting systems, fines and penalties are charged to the individual's phone bill each month. In some jurisdictions, private collection bureaus are used. Special court calendars may be set up solely to enforce payment of financial sanctions.

Financial sanctions are popular with legislators and the voting public. The idea of offenders literally paying for their crimes is very appealing to many. Consequently, there will probably continue to be an expansion in the number and kinds of monetary obligations imposed on convicted offenders. Nevertheless, the inability of the individual to pay and the cost to collect are factors often overlooked. Supervision agencies borrow successful collection techniques from the private sector and should try other innovative methods.

Drug Testing

Drug testing is often used to monitor offender compliance with substance abuse prohibitions in most conditional release corrections programs. Technology in this area has undergone significant improvement during recent years and is currently available in a variety of types and modalities for easy use by program staff.

Blood testing for the presence of drugs has been common for many years, but it is a costly and time-consuming method that usually requires trained medical staff. Therefore, urine monitoring is now frequently used to determine whether offenders have ingested selected drugs within a relatively short period (three to four days). Urine samples may be collected within an office facility and then analyzed by program staff or sent to an outside laboratory or remote locations through drug-specific cassettes that provide immediate identification of drugs. Because of these advantages, urinalysis has become commonplace in community corrections as the testing methodology of choice.

Drug testing is a rapidly evolving forensic field. In recent years, hair and saliva tests have been explored as effective monitoring alternatives. Hair testing permits the supervising agency to examine for the use of certain drugs over an extended time period up to six months or more. Unfortunately, hair analysis through radioimmunoassay technology is expensive, a factor that often limits use of this noninvasive approach by corrections. Saliva testing is another promising approach. Although it is as accurate as urinalysis, it is only effective for detecting drug use within a few hours. Voice recognition (e.g., identifying participants by means of voice modulation techniques) is another new strategy for determining the use of drugs, but like its newer counterparts, it lacks the development of appropriate standard measures for comparative analysis.

Outpatient and Residential Treatment Facilities

A widely held orientation to the genesis of illegal behavior tends to view much of it as related to mental, emotional, and behavioral maladjustments. These "problems," like physical maladies, can be diagnosed, treated, and cured. The vehicle for delivering the requisite services is the treatment facility. There the various categories of nonphysical illnesses can be dissected and analyzed to determine the underlying causes, the precipitating incidents, the developmental history, and the prognosis. Proper techniques can be used to produce conformity to social norms.

Substance abuse is high on the list of "causal" factors related to crime. In addition to the illegal activities of possession, use, and sales, intoxication by drugs or alcohol leads to a wide variety of socially unacceptable behaviors. Further, mental and emotional maladjustment or developmental aberrations lead to other kinds of interactions considered undesirable and therefore made illegal by laws that act to shape and maintain the moral fabric of society. Sexual and violent acting-out are just two forms in which anomalies are expressed.

Treatment facilities attempt to alleviate these problems through rehabilitative efforts. The organizations and their physical plants may address a wide variety of issues or focus narrowly on one or two. Some substance abuse programs may deal exclusively with either drugs or alcohol, while others include both kinds of addiction. Still others further specialize in specific types of drugs (e.g., crack cocaine or heroine).

The mental health field in general is equally as diverse. Some centers and programs may attempt to treat a broad spectrum of mental and emotional problems while others specialize in a certain area, such as domestic abuse, child molestation, rape and assault, adjustment problems, psychopathic manifestations, kleptomania, and so forth. Treatment plans often include a mixture of individual therapy, group counseling, self-help or support groups, legal drugs for the control of unacceptable behavior and/or other symptoms, and a host of other specialized treatments and therapies. Support groups for family members and significant others are common.

This plethora of treatment modalities is packaged many different ways. However, the two main categories are residential and outpatient. The former takes in offenders considered to be high risk either to themselves or to others. They need to be kept away from the public, under observation, and involved with intensive therapy. The ordinary cares of living in the community and being responsible for one's own maintenance are eliminated. Energy and attention are focused on addressing mental, emotional, and interactional problems.

For those who have better impulse control and the capacity to look after all or most of their creature needs and who are not dangerous to themselves and others, outpatient treatment is the modality of choice. Costs are a fraction of live-in situations. Lifestyle is closer to the routine of the average citizen. Growth and development take place within the context of the community with its attendant demands and resources.

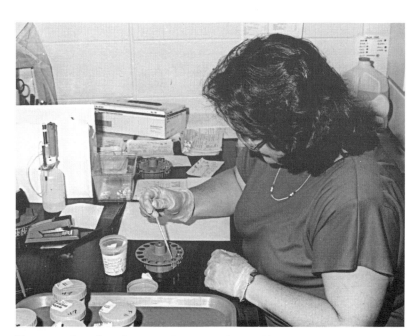

Drug testing is often used to monitor offender compliance with substance abuse prohibitions.

51

Either residential or outpatient care may be ordered as a condition of the sentence imposed by the court or set up by the paroling authorities. Ensuring compliance is the role of the supervising officer; failure to follow the conditions may result in revocation hearings and resentencing.

Spatial and Time Liberty Restrictions

Selected intermediate sanction programs provide significant limitations on offender involvement within the community. The purpose of such restrictions regulating the participant's freedom of motion is to provide an element of punishment and encourage law-abiding behavior by keeping offenders out of harm's way. At its least intrusive level, the programs set curfews prescribing the time periods during which the offender must be at a designated residence unless alternative arrangements have been approved previously by staff or the controlling authority of the courts or parole boards.

More restrictive spatial and time limitations include periods of home detention and house arrest. Home detention sanctions specify circumscribed periods of time during which the offender is prohibited from leaving a designated residence. These time periods usually range from one to seven days and often include weekends. House arrest programs define a longer period, often weeks or months, of limitation to the home site. Frequently, these restrictions are modified to allow for employment or counseling.

Electronic monitoring of these conditions helps staff ensure compliance. Monitoring techniques may serve as an alternative or an adjunct to curfew visits, but to be effective they must be augmented by offender supervision (e.g., remedial efforts to assist offenders in complying with the conditions of their sentence). The major forms of electronic monitoring include passive and radio frequency systems. Passive systems depend on telephone contact with offenders who may be required to respond verbally or to place a wristlet, anklet, or necklace into a confirmation device attached to the telephone. Frequently, the calls are computer-generated, have set calling periods, and recall whenever contact is not made.

The radio frequency method uses technology requiring offenders to remain within a specified geographical limit, usually 200 feet, of a base station that itself is a computer. The base station records all violations of the established perimeters (often allowing time away for work and counseling) and reports by telephone to a host computer. Radio frequency systems can be augmented with "patrol by" techniques that allow officers to ensure the offender is at home by driving by the residence and receiving a verification report from the base computer.

There have been extensive advances in electronic monitoring technology, which provides a means for remote drug testing. Videophones are one of the newest technologies now available to provide pictures of participants over telephone lines to ensure compliance with geographical and spatial conditions.

Intensive Supervision Programs

Intensive supervision programs (ISPs) provide increased monitoring of offenders residing within the community. Such supervision attempts to limit offender risk by enhancing surveillance and control by reducing caseloads, increasing offender-officer contact, requiring punitive or remedial elements, and restricting the range of permitted offender activities. ISPs are often coupled with required community service, drug monitoring and treatment, compulsory employment, remedial education, curfews, electronic monitoring, financial sanctions, and selected counseling activities. Although contact rates vary dramatically among jurisdictions, most ISPs require levels of contact ranging from weekly to daily communication. Staff members are often assigned caseloads individually but may act in teams with other professionals, paraprofessionals, or community members. Many ISPs are characterized by a substantial proportion of the staff's work being completed during nontraditional work hours, including evenings and weekends.

ISPs may be developed as "front end" options that permit initial sentencing or rapid resentencing to the program by judges. They may also serve as "back door" approaches by permitting inmates, prior to parole, to spend a portion of their institutional sentence in ISP as a prerequisite to a parole determination. In either case, substantive violations of the conditions of ISP usually result in a prison or jail term. Sometimes perceived as an alternative to incarceration, ISPs attempt to demonstrate cost-effectiveness by comparing operating expenditures to institutional expenses while comparative recidivism studies show significantly better results.

Recent research on the effectiveness of ISPs demonstrates the need to incorporate not only increased surveillance techniques but also reintegration programs that include drug and other counseling services, employment, and community support if they are to succeed. Failure to manage offenders in a comprehensive way dealing with both their risks and needs tends to lead to a higher rate of technical violations with no significant change in recidivism levels.

Day Reporting Centers

A relatively recent addition to the panoply of intermediate sanctions is the day reporting center (DRC). Offenders are required to report physically to a designated community-based facility each day and participate in a highly structured set of activities. Often, conditions of release to DRCs include a specified daily community service sanction, required drug testing, employment searches, remedial education, life skills training, vocational instruction, and specialized group or individual counseling. A typical day at a DRC may be structured with community service in the morning, employment-related training and job searches in the afternoon, and specialized counseling or remedial education in the evening.

DRC approaches vary widely among jurisdictions and may function Monday through Friday, 9:00 a.m. to 5:00 p.m.; some operate twenty-four hours, seven days a week. Often participants are provided with a telephone call-in schedule, a curfew, and an electronic monitoring apparatus. DRC may also be part of a larger intermediate sanctioning scheme and may fit between an intensive supervision approach and a halfway house. In some jurisdictions, DRC participants move through set stages and receive greater freedom and self-directed activity as rewards for compliant behavior.

Restitution Centers

During the 1980s and early 1990s, growing attention has been paid to the need to compensate victims for both monetary losses and medical expenses incurred as a result of the commission of a crime. In many states, legislation provides for the payment of penalty assessments to special programs designed to assist victims of violent offenses. Laws requiring offenders to pay fines, drug fees, laboratory costs, and a myriad other financial sanctions have forced community corrections agencies to expand their collection operations significantly and make them more effective.

Most offenders are sentenced to pay such assessments as a condition of traditional probation or parole activities. Research continues to demonstrate that with appropriate accounting and computer support, a majority of probationers and parolees pay some or all of their court-ordered fees. A small percentage, however, continue to resist paying because they are unemployed or otherwise

do not have sufficient funds to meet their obligations. In some jurisdictions, restitution centers have been established. There, offenders are required to participate in a highly structured residential program that combines community service, remedial education, and special counseling with job-seeking skills, vocational education, and employment. The emphasis of these programs is to help offenders secure and maintain employment and to meet financial sanctions. Many programs also require offenders to pay a dedicated portion of their income for their maintenance in the restitution center. Stays in the center are typically of short duration. Early release may be earned by securing employment and establishing wage attachments and other means of paying the obligation.

Weekend Detention/Jail

Weekend detention programs have developed throughout the United States, affording sentencing judges the option to provide an element of punitiveness to a sentence while minimizing some of the negative consequences normally attached to incarceration. Defendants receiving such a sanction are typically required to appear at the correctional facility Friday evening and are released sometime late on Sunday. Sentences usually stipulate the number of weekends or total number of days to be served. Often these sentences are handed down when the defendant has committed a nonviolent offense, has ties in the community, and is employed.

The structure of the weekend sentence varies among jurisdictions. Some defendants spend their entire weekend within the jail facility, partaking of normal institutional

Weekend detention programs provide an element of punitiveness to a sentence while minimalizing the negative consequences usually associated with incarceration.

activities. Others simply remain "behind bars" in a penitentiary mode. Other defendants join group community service sites during the day and spend their evenings in the jail. With the specter of jail crowding hanging over their heads, some corrections administrators have developed modified weekend detention, permitting a combination of community service and electronic monitoring to substitute for jail time. Others simply provide jail credits for defendants who appear at the facility on Friday evenings without institutionalization.

Weekend detention sanctions are often combined with other supervision requirements, such as financial penalties, drug testing, community service, and required counseling. Some ISPs use weekend detention periods as a punitive aspect in response to technical violations rather than returning the offender for revocation. In general, however, these sentences are used for first-time, minor, or nonviolent offenders who, the judges determine, need a "punitive bite" without the full effects of incarceration.

Halfway Houses

Halfway house programs provide a prerelease mechanism from prison. Typically, a preparole period is authorized by corrections authorities to permit selected inmates with positive institutional records to be released into a non-secure facility prior to their scheduled parole date. Time spent at the halfway house includes provisions for counseling, remedial education, job skills training, and facility upkeep. Participants complying with institutional rules regarding structured community living arrangements are permitted to secure employment outside the institution. Opportunity for gradual increases in self-direction are afforded to inmates, permitting them greater command over their own lives. Curfews, weekend passes, and furloughs are often provided as positive rewards for program compliance.

As increased periods of personal control are provided within halfway house environments, individual and specialized counseling programs are developed to help offenders remain crime-free in the community. Drug testing is often a mandatory condition of release. Successful completion of the halfway house program may be a prerequisite for parole.

Such institutionally based programs, whether publicly or privately administered, are occasionally referred to as halfway "out" houses. In contrast, offenders are place in halfway "in" houses prior to a sentence of incarceration. Judges are provided with the option of a short-term, controlled facility that provides both a punitive and a rehabilitative element to the sentence. Eligibility require-

ments, length of stay, program elements, and release mechanisms vary among states.

Halfway in houses may also be used for probation and parole violators as a means to serve notice that change must come about in their behavior or it surely will come in the status of their freedom. Punitive elements are coupled with programs designed for constructive change. If this approach is successful, violators avoid violation hearings and more restrictive outcomes are reserved for those who cannot be successful within the confinement of a halfway house program.

Boot Camp

Military-style boot camps represent a growing effort to combine the incapacitative effects of institutionalization with efforts to promote discipline and good physical health. Typically, as an alternative to prison, young adult institutions, or training schools, such programs provide a two- to six-month term of rigorous, physical conditioning combined with group activities, short hair cuts, drill and ceremony, and a regimented lifestyle. Institutional terms are relatively short and may or may not be combined with an aftercare program.

Participant selection criteria vary among the jurisdictions as do control (judiciary or correctional department), duration, aftercare components, release mechanisms, and counseling modalities. As a form of short-term incarceration, boot camp theory holds that a brief institutionalization followed by a highly regimented series of self-improvement steps, an increase in self-esteem, and hard manual labor will lead the participant to a law-abiding lifestyle.

Most boot camps developed since the 1980s include significant remedial education components, drug counseling, and vocational skills. These elements are designed to assist offenders after graduation and release into the community. Boot camp programs also provide aftercare elements that range from intensive supervision to periodic assistance for graduates.

Recently, significant federal attention has been paid to this form of "shock incarceration." Grant funds and technical assistance in program design and implementation have been made available to sites interested in exploring this sanction. Although the effectiveness of boot camps remains a controversial topic, significant evaluative research is underway to help guide future program development.

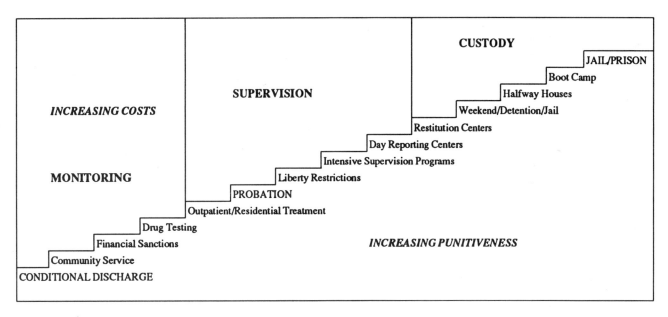

Figure 1. STEP PARADIGM

Policy Directions for the Future

The development and proliferation of a wide variety of community-based criminal justice interventions, such as the selections described in this chapter, do not in themselves constitute a program of intermediate sanctions. Fundamentally, intermediate sanctions ought to be a statement of policy, that is, a comprehensive plan developed by government setting forth specific correctional goals and designing objectives to reach them. Within an intermediate sanctions sentencing policy, there should be a clear delineation of the variety and scope of programs to be enacted as the means to reach goals and objectives. The types of offenders to be managed within each program should be specified. The concept of a graduated range of sanctions is broad enough to encompass the identification of particular correctional options designed to meet community and offender needs while outlining a mechanism to permit complying offenders to earn lower levels of supervision and recalcitrant ones to have their sanctions "racheted up." In short, offenders who perform well should be rewarded while those who fail must be subject to increasing levels of control if society is to be protected. As these options are graded against scales of punitiveness and intrusiveness into offender lives, a "step" paradigm begins to evolve (see Figure 1).

Too often discussions concerning intermediate sanctions become bogged down in attempts to determine if the resulting programs are "alternatives to incarceration" or "enhancements of traditional probation." In addition, there are concerns over net-widening—subjecting people who ordinarily would have received traditional probation to more restrictive sentences, such as prison, halfway houses, or ISPs. Although these issues are legitimate discussion points regarding intermediate sanctions sentencing policy, they should not be determinative in setting the approach. Rather, the various branches of government, *together* with community representatives, should attempt to set firm, clear policy and program goals by which the selection of the appropriate sentencing components should be made for each offender or class of offenders. The key is being clear about intent, purpose, and ultimate short- and long-term aims.

Recent research by the Public Agenda Foundation demonstrated the willingness of communities to embrace the intermediate sanctions concept. In Alabama and Delaware, groups of citizens were brought together to discuss and select sentences for hypothetical offenders. After an education program on intermediate sanctions, the groups again "sentenced" the offenders to incarceration, probation, or intermediate sanctions. In both jurisdictions, the groups overwhelmingly supported intermediate sanction programs after being informed about their intent and effect.

The Center for Effective Public Policy has been assisting jurisdictions throughout the United States in developing individual intermediate sanctions policies. They suggest that there are at least six essential elements in the process of developing intermediate sanctions:

- an identified and organized work group to develop policy

- good base-line information to establish structure, decision points, areas of discretion, and trends

- a continuing process of goal and outcome clarification

- a system-scanning capability to find and use existing data and to analyze and evaluate alternative proposals

- ongoing review of the policies and practices of individual agencies

- policy creation and implementation

Perhaps two more elements should be included in this list. First, the planning group should offer an opportunity for meaningful public involvement. After all, intermediate sanctions should be developed for the public, and therefore its members should be specifically included to represent its values, interests, and concerns. "Community" corrections needs to be responsive to the trends of public opinion and ought to inspire confidence that the community is being protected. Citizen involvement will create a feeling of ownership and will ensure public support even when inevitable occasional failures are encountered.

Finally, an independent mechanism must be created to monitor and evaluate the effectiveness of the intermediate sanctioning policy and its component parts. Too often the results of community corrections programs are ambiguous and open to subjective interpretations. Many probation and parole professionals have their personal opinions about which programs work best for which groups of offenders. Also, in many situations, perceived program effectiveness for particular target populations is not as influential in sentencing decisions as what is expedient, politically astute, popular, or available.

To be truly effective, a uniform program of independent sanctions must use sound research methodology to document which populations benefit most from each of the components of the broad spectrum of sentencing options. Behavior change, pre- and postprogram differences in illegal activities, and community protection must also be considered. Results-oriented evaluations will bolster public support, reinforce judicial decisions, and stipulate constructive changes in supervision techniques. When clear, realistic goals and objectives are associated with stringent performance measures, an effective and unified program of intermediate sanctions will emerge.

References

American Probation and Parole Association. 1991. *American Probation and Parole Association's drug testing guidelines and practices for adult probation and parole agencies.* Washington, D.C.: U.S. Department of Justice, Bureau of Justice Assistance.

Bureau of Justice Statistics, 1983. *Sourcebook of criminal justice statistics—1983.* Washington, D.C.: U.S. Department of Justice.

Bureau of Justice Statistics. 1991. *Sourcebook of criminal justice statistics—1991.* Washington, D.C.: U.S. Department of Justice.

Center for Effective Public Policy. n.d. *Improving the use of intermediate sanctions: Lessons from the intermediate sanctions project.* Washington. D.C.: Center for Effective Public Policy.

APPLICABLE ACA STANDARDS

Standards for Adult Probation and Parole Field Services
  Administration, Organization, and Management 2-3011, 2-3012
  Fiscal Management 2-3081
  Supervision—Probation and Parole Agencies 2-3123, 2-3129, 2-3130, 2-3132, 2-3149
  Supervision—Parole Agencies Only 2-3172, 2-3177
  Supervision—Probation Agencies Only 2-3182, 2-3183

7

Electronic Monitoring

By Mario A. Paparozzi

Some form of electronic monitoring (EM) of offenders has existed in the United States since 1964, when research scientists in Massachusetts conducted an experiment in which a portable tracking device was used to monitor the location of parolees and mental patients. This experiment—which continued through 1970—was not initiated nor was it endorsed by criminal justice policymakers.

On completion of the Massachusetts experiment, there was little or no interest expressed by corrections officials in actually implementing a form of EM of offenders. At the time, little external pressure was put on corrections officials to explore alternatives to traditional incarceration.

As sentencing laws changed and prison populations burgeoned to crisis proportions during the 1980s, increased pressures came to bear on legislators and corrections officials to find cost-effective alternatives to prisons and jails. The first state to use EM was New Mexico in 1983. In 1984, Florida implemented an EM program. Both of these programs were for probationers, and both were considered successful by the practitioners who designed and implemented them.

As Florida and New Mexico's initial success became known to corrections officials around the country, other correctional policymakers became interested in exploring this seemingly cost-effective solution to their prison crowding problems. Today, virtually every state has an EM program or plans to develop one. The uses of EM in these jurisdictions are diverse. They can be part of pretrial,

probation, parole, work release, institutional furlough, or jail/prison programs.

These programs are implemented on the federal, state, and local levels. In some quarters, EM has been viewed as an electronic jail of sorts. Manufacturers of EM equipment attempted to gain market share and expand use of their products by arguing that this new technology is inexpensive compared with the costs of incarceration. Equipment manufacturers have also contended that EM is effective when used as an enhancement to probation and parole supervision programs. In this regard, many of the new generation intensive supervision programs have used EM as an aid to supervision. It should be noted that EM programs are implemented on the federal, state, and local levels.

The past ten years of experience with EM have shown that it is not the panacea it was originally thought to be. Even most of the major manufacturers of EM equipment are now quick to point out the limitations of the technology. Practitioners argue that EM is only as good as the program in which it is used. In short, no technology, including EM, will make up for the deficits of a bad programmatic concept or design. Like many other criminal justice programs and technologies, EM suffers from the same lack of thoughtful assessment regarding its efficacy by the general public.

There are two basic types of technology that drive EM: passive and active. Both technologies require the use of telecommunications. The use of the telephone, however, for each of the technologies is distinctly different.

Mario A. Paparozzi, treasurer of the American Probation and Parole Association, is assistant chief for the New Jersey Bureau of Parole.

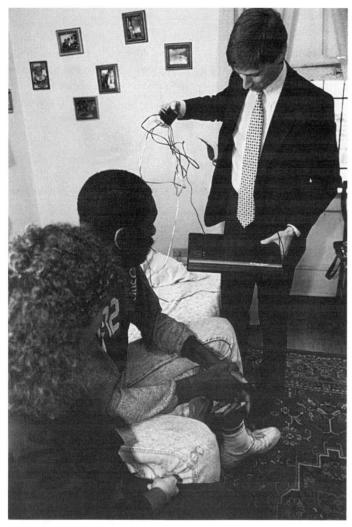

As technology advances, transmitters and other equipment used in electronic monitoring are becoming less obtrusive and offer more options. *(Officer standing.)*

Passive Technology

In a passive system, the telephone is used to make calls at designated intervals to an offender's home. The telephone calls are generated by a central computer. Passive systems are alternatively known as "programmed contact" systems, because telephone contacts with the offender are made according to a computer-generated phone call schedule. Programmed contact systems monitor offenders only during times when telephone calls are made from a central computer. The central computer is an ordinary personal computer configuration.

Passive systems are designed to reduce labor intensiveness in the event the offender's phone is not answered

(e.g., if a busy signal occurs, if there is an operator intercept, or there is some other problem with the phone lines). The central computer can generate automatic phone calls back to the offender's home. The time lapse between phone calls as well as the frequency of callbacks is flexible and is programmed into the central computer.

Verification of the offender's presence or absence at the location of the receiving telephone is made in one of several ways.

Voice Verification

Voice verification has been used with some success, although it has accuracy problems. In controlled laboratory settings, voice-verification technology has been shown to be 80 to 90 percent accurate. In practical applications, the accuracy rates have been less successful. This type of system does not require the offender to wear a transmitting device. Voice-verification technology requires creating an offender's voice print and storing that print in a central computer.

Visual Verification

Another verification technology uses a combination of video and telecommunications technology. Systems based on this technology transmit a still photograph to a central computer and/or video monitor. To further ensure an offender's actual presence at the time of the photo transmission, the offender is given instructions at random during each phone call to touch an ear, nose, etc. Like voice verification, this technology does not require the offender to wear a transmitter.

Encoded Digital Verification

Another passive verification technology is one based on an encoded transmission that is made when a transmitter (worn by the offender) is inserted into a matched verifier device. The verifier device is connected to a central computer via telephone lines. When a random phone call is made to an offender's home, the offender is asked to insert the transmitter into the verifier. When correctly inserted, the central computer is notified that a "good handshake" has occurred. If the offender does not insert the transmitter properly, the computer will be so notified and another phone call may be automatically generated.

Advantages and Disadvantages

Most passive technologies have the advantage of avoiding the need for an offender to actually wear a transmitter. It has been argued that wearing a transmitter can stigmatize the offender. Although stigmatization may be a concern, it is minimized by wearing the transmitter under clothing. Additionally, transmitters used with passive-only systems are significantly smaller than transmitters that include active or radio frequency components. As the state of EM advances, it is likely that transmitters will become even less obtrusive.

Passive systems have the disadvantage of requiring a number of telephone calls to an offender's home. Some offenders and their families have complained about the disruption of numerous telephone calls, especially during the late-night hours. Of course, the frequency of phone calls could be reduced. These kinds of decisions, however, must be balanced against the agency's supervision requirements for the type of offender assigned to the EM program.

Active Technology

Active technology involves a continuous signaling system. Continuous signaling systems, unlike passive or programmed contact systems, provide continuous monitoring of the offender. This type of system minimally comprises a transmitting unit, a home monitor and receiver unit, and a central computer/receiver unit. The transmitter is usually strapped to the offender's ankle, although in some instances, it is strapped to the offender's wrist. Placement of the wrist or ankle transmitter is determined by the design of the equipment being used, the agency's desires, and the offender's needs. The transmitter operates on a specially designed battery that requires replacement from time to time. The frequency of battery replacement varies by manufacturer.

The transmitter broadcasts a radio frequency signal to the receiver, which is located in the offender's home. The radio frequency signal is coded to work with the receiver so that another transmitter cannot confound the integrity of the monitoring equipment. The receiver in the offender's home is connected by telephone to the central computer. When the offender wearing the transmitter is within range of the home monitor (receiving unit), there is an indication at the central computer that the offender is at home. When the offender goes beyond the range of transmission, the radio frequency signal is not received by the home receiver, and the central system records the offender as not present.

The normal range a transmitter will successfully communicate with the receiver is 100 to 150 feet. The range can be affected by the location of the receiving unit in the offender's home (e.g., if the unit is low to the ground or behind an appliance). Building construction and the strength of the battery in the transmitter itself are other factors that affect the integrity of the transmission.

The central computer to which the receiver is telephonically linked is used to program time parameters for periods of home confinement. This principle also applies to systems based on passive technology. Periods of home confinement can be customized to the needs of supervision. The central system will continually monitor the presence or absence of an offender even during periods of authorized leave from the residence. A running computer printout can be generated and/or the data can be stored on floppy diskettes.

Another type of active system does not involve telecommunications. This type of system requires the offender to wear a standard transmitter and the supervising agent to carry a portable receiver, either on his or her person or in the car. The portable receiver will receive the signal from the transmitter when the transmitter is within range. This kind of a monitoring system is useful for verifying the presence or absence of an offender at work, at a treatment program, and so forth.

The latest development of this technology has set the stage for its increased use in supervising a group of offenders, at one time, in community settings. For example, one supervising agent can supervise a group with a portable receiver that receives radio frequency transmissions from a group of offenders—each wearing a transmitter that is uniquely encoded to the portable receiver. If an offender goes beyond acceptable range, the receiver indicates a problem.

Hybrid Systems

Many manufacturers offer hybrid systems. A hybrid system integrates a standard, continuous signal, radio frequency system with a programmed contact passive system. The applications of a hybrid system vary. The system can be stand-alone radio frequency, stand-alone automated programmed contact, or completely integrated.

If, for example, an implementing agency desires a less restrictive and potentially less costly form of monitoring, it may opt to place offenders on a programmed contact form of supervision after they have successfully completed a period of supervision under the radio frequency system. Hybrid systems provide the flexibility of automated calls to the offender whenever a radio frequency problem is detected. The programmed contact system serves as a backup to radio frequency in this situation. Automated calls and positive verification of the offender's presence obviate the need for human intervention in many instances.

Hybrid systems provide a mechanism to monitor offenders in the event electrical lines are out of service. Power outages can and do occur that cause an interruption in electrical power. When this occurs, phone lines often can still function. Passive systems can monitor offenders when this kind of a situation occurs.

Tamper-proof Bands

All monitoring bands used with EM equipment can be forcibly removed by the wearer. As it is discussed here, "tamper-proof" means that the central computer will indicate a tamper if the offender attempts to stretch or otherwise damage the band. Some less expensive systems offer this detection element. Agencies that use nontamper-proof bands rely on frequent visual inspections to detect problems.

Tamper-proof bands provide instant notification of a problem, which allows implementing agencies to respond immediately. Immediate responses are important and not just for surveillance or enforcement reasons. Immediate

responses enhance the ability of agencies to effect positive behavioral change.

Matching Equipment to Program Model

Community-based corrections programs that use EM must not lose sight of the purpose of the program. Too often EM programs become focused on surveillance or monitoring activities to the exclusion of intervention. EM provides the ability to conduct "state-of-the-art watching" of offenders. This alone will do little to control behavior in the short or long term. Appropriately designed, EM programs are both community-based as well as community-placed. Programs that focus exclusively on surveillance may indeed be community-placed but are not community-corrections-based in terms of their goals or guiding paradigm.

There are many different program models. The implementing agency must design its ideal program model, including specific results-oriented objectives. EM should be viewed as a technology that will support the program model and specific program objectives. EM is not the "silver bullet" that corrections officials and the public are looking for to solve the burgeoning crime and prison crowding problems. It is an adjunct to supervision.

Accuracy of EM equipment is important not only for surveillance purposes, it is also important if the program is designed to provide an immediate response to violations. The ability to provide an immediate response can be used to teach new behavior to offenders, especially youthful offenders and offenders with addictive personalities.

Depending on the program model, certain decisions must be made about the type of EM system that will best serve the program. The program model should drive the selection of the technology to be used. In some instances, programs may be designed to fit a particular type of technology. As long as the goals of effective intervention are served, this is not problematic. If the goals of the intervention process are defined *a priori*, then the path to an appropriate technology will be clear.

New monitoring bands worn by offenders are small and discreet.

Custody programs often require the continuous monitoring capability active radio frequency systems provide. In these cases, the program model requires restricted movement of the offender during certain time frames. Less restrictive programs may meet their objectives by using a programmed-contact type of system. Some models use a combination of radio frequency and programmed contacts, depending on the offender's adjustment in the community.

Electronic Monitoring for Rewards and Relapses

In corrections the word "sanction" is typically used as a synonym to "punishment." Electronically monitored periods of home confinement can be used as an intermediate punishment. When offenders assigned to an electronically monitored supervision program do not comply with conditions of a case plan, curfews can be restricted. Conversely, curfew schedules can be expanded as a reward for good behavior.

Too often, programs fail to develop reward systems for good behavior. The focus of community corrections programs is, unfortunately, frequently on negative responses to program violations. EM need not, and should not, be limited to a punishment perspective. EM can assist in teaching new behavior to offenders, and it can facilitate the relapse prevention process.

EM can also be useful as a relapse prevention strategy. There may be times during an offender's community adjustment process when more structure will prevent lapses into undesirable behavior. EM provides a mechanism for such structure.

Drawbacks

As is the case of probation and parole programs in general, legislators, judges, and the public often have some misconceptions about program operations. There are many variations in program design for community corrections programs involving EM; however, there is a tendency to group all programs together. This becomes problematic for practitioners when a particular program experiences problems (e.g., a crime committed by a participant in the program). Criticisms are often levied at the entire concept of EM rather than the specific program involved.

Also, there is a wide variation in the offender profile of participants placed in EM programs. Some programs, for example, are designed to be open for business during traditional business hours. In these programs, a violation that occurs after hours is typically discovered the next business day and is responded to at that time. Other programs are far more stringent in their supervision requirements. These programs may, for example, confine offenders in their homes around the clock and respond to violations immediately, regardless of the time of day. Obviously the difference in program design will account for some of the outcome experiences.

Because of the high visibility in the media of EM programs, crimes committed by program participants are likely to receive widespread coverage. As a result, program operators are inclined to assign to EM programs cases that are most likely to succeed. Typically, offenders with a history of violence are excluded from EM programs. Some programs exclude drug dealers and users.

Yet, high-risk offenders benefit most from intensive services and supervision. Placing low-risk offenders in intensive programs with EM can actually exacerbate prison crowding problems. Given that intensive supervision programs with EM can cost as much as three to five times more than traditional forms of probation and parole (Byrne, Lurigio & Baird 1989), assigning offenders at least risk to this state-of-the-art supervision technology and those of highest risk to general, albeit less visible, supervision becomes problematic.

Bureaucrats have become increasingly cautious about the client profile of those who are to be electronically monitored. Unfortunately, the use of EM for low-risk offenders does not serve public safety interests. It should be overtly acknowledged that no correctional option (including and especially prison) is 100 percent successful in terms of recidivism rates (however defined). The best that can be done is to try to increase the odds for short-term control and longer term behavioral reform of offenders. EM can and must be used as something more than a device to divert low-risk offenders from jails and prisons. Additional benefits will certainly be realized if EM is used in the context of meaningful supervision to offenders who are high-risk and being released to probation and parole programs in significant numbers on a daily basis.

Reference

Byrne, J., A. Lurigio, and C. Baird. 1989. The effectiveness of the new intensive supervision programs. *Research in Corrections* (2): 1–56.

8

Drug Testing in Probation and Parole Supervision

By Edward Tedder

Drug abuse continues to be a widespread problem in the United States. Everyday, courts and parole boards wrestle over decisions about which offenders should be placed on probation or parole and returned to the community. The drug dilemma has compelled probation and parole administrators to take a different approach in supervision strategies for many offenders under their supervision. One strategy is drug testing. In the past, offenders involved with drugs were referred to outside agencies or service providers for drug testing services, but now, more and more probation and parole agencies are assuming these functions.

The law allows the criminal justice system to require drug testing as a condition of probation or parole. Drug testing is considered reasonable as long as the circumstances are not arbitrary and the purpose of the drug test is related to conviction or rehabilitation (*U.S. v. Williams*, 787 F2d 1182 CA7 1986).

Drug testing should have specific goals or objectives and is most effective when it is used in conjunction with other supervision and management strategies. Drug testing, whether conducted by outside agencies, probation and parole agencies, or a combination of the two, provides probation and parole agencies with a vital tool for achieving their goals and objectives in the supervision and management of drug-involved offenders.

Edward Tedder is the former training and technical assistance manager for the American Probation and Parole Association.

Although a number of methods are available for detecting drug abuse, the one most widely accepted by the courts is urinalysis. Although some consider urinalysis as a drug-detecting tool intrusive, it is popular because probation and parole staff do not need extensive training or clinical experience to perform these tests.

Role of Drug Testing in Supervision

Drug testing is one of the best tools available to probation and parole agencies for monitoring and controlling offenders' behavior. It can be effective in individual case management, management of targeted populations, and detection and tracking of drug abuse trends within established jurisdictions.

Goals and objectives among probation and parole agencies differ according to each agency's mission. However, most include the following fundamental components:

- identification
- assessment
- case planning
- deterrence
- surveillance

Field officer training often includes instruction on using drug tests.

Probation and parole agencies need to understand how drug testing can extend the functional roles of each of these components. Awareness of its usefulness in developing and managing supervision goals and objectives for the offender is also critical. Central to identification, assessment, and case management is the element of early intervention with the drug-involved offender. The degree of success achieved with the drug-involved offender is highly dependent on how well each of these supervision elements are coordinated and managed.

Identification

Drug testing can be used to identify drug-involved offenders, the drugs they are abusing, and drug-use patterns within a given community or probation and parole population. Most drug abusers, particularly those under probation or parole supervision, will not admit to using illicit drugs.

However, when properly conducted, drug testing can break through offender denial. Drug testing helps identify the presence or absence of illicit drugs and serves as a source of documentation regarding an offender's compliance with conditions set forth by the court, parole board, or probation department.

Assessment

Drug testing can be used to assess offenders' drugs of choice, extent of use and involvement, and ability to abstain from use. By doing so, drug testing can help determine the most appropriate drug intervention or treatment strategy.

Case Planning

Case planning is essential for measuring an offender's progress while under supervision. Data from drug testing are important when developing supervision and case management plans for individuals and specific offender populations. Drug testing may be combined with other available resources as a tool for determining risk levels, supervision requirements, and appropriate offender treatment and rehabilitative services.

Deterrence

Drug testing serves as a deterrent when offenders realize that they may be tested with little or no prior notice, that tests are accurate and reliable, and that a positive test may result in punitive proceedings. Moreover, drug testing can lead offenders to admit to drug use and provide an incentive for remaining drug-free.

Surveillance

Drug testing supports surveillance efforts when it is used to monitor compliance with conditions of supervision. It also indicates other factors that may affect offender behavior.

Using Drug Testing Successfully

To ensure drug testing is used effectively, probation and parole agencies need to identify their specific drug testing goals and objectives. These may include all or any combination of the five components addressed in the previous section. Whichever components are selected, a number of questions must be answered, including: Who should be tested? When should testing be conducted? What drugs should be tested?

Responses to these questions will vary according to the purpose for which drug testing is established. The following are vital to the successful use of drug testing:

1. Develop and implement clear and succinctly written policies and procedures governing the use of drug testing.

2. Select appropriate offender population(s) for testing.

3. Select drug testing methodology(ies) that best serve the agency's needs and resources.

4. Establish reasonable protocol for when, how often, and what drugs should be tested.

5. Ensure reliable and defensible confirmation procedures are used when appropriate.

6. Ensure proper chain-of-custody procedures are observed.

7. Develop stringent controls pertaining to reporting and sharing results.

8. Follow judicious and expedient procedures for how drug test results are used.

Policies and Procedures

Agencies should develop and implement clear and succinctly written policies and procedures that govern drug testing practices. Policies and procedures formalize drug testing goals and objectives and provide a framework for policy implementation. They help to ensure program direction, understanding, and unity of purpose. Furthermore, a written policy promotes consistency and continuity during program implementation and during periods of transition. Policies and procedures should clearly identify and define the roles, responsibilities, and functions of program personnel. Provisions should be made allowing for policy revision and objective evaluation of policy effectiveness, preferably by outside sources.

Offender Selection

The process of selecting offenders for testing is vital to agency drug testing programs. Often, budget or logistical considerations compel agencies to limit the number of offender categories or populations tested. Criteria need to be established specifying who is to be tested and at what stages of supervision. A risk and needs assessment, coupled with other evaluation instruments, can furnish appropriate requisites for this decision-making process. Frequently, the courts or other decision-making authorities will identify who is to be tested.

Developing and implementing an appropriate assessment process can reduce the overall costs associated with drug testing. Assessments or reassessments may occur at any time during the offender's supervision. Reassessments may require modifying existing testing requirements.

Drug Testing Methodology

Prior to selecting a drug testing methodology, agencies should review and identify specific drug testing requirements. The methodology selected should correspond with the purpose and mission of the agency. It may be necessary for probation and parole agencies to select more than one methodology, depending on the program's design.

Immunoassay is the primary methodology for conducting all initial drug tests. Immunoassay is a testing process that uses antibodies to detect the presence of drugs. Each immunoassay has antibodies that respond only to the particular drug or drug metabolites (substance resulting in breakdown of a drug in the body) for which a test is run. Tests may be performed by probation or parole staff on location (probation or parole office) or other suitable and available locations or by outside contracted laboratories certified to conduct tests for drug abuse.

Testing Protocol

Offenders may be selected for testing during the presentence investigation, intake, or agency assessment phase, and/or as a condition of probation or parole.

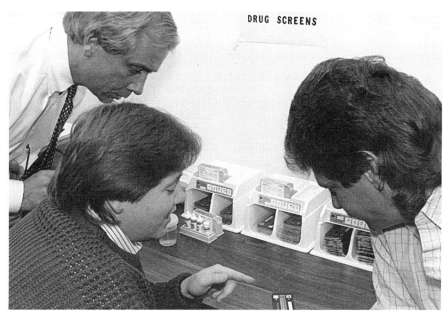

Trained officers can apply drug testing screens when the offender comes in for an office visit. *(Officers on the left.)*

Agencies should follow an established selection criteria concerning who should be tested and at what stages of supervision. Typically, agencies test offenders who are under supervision as a result of a drug or drug-related offense, who have a prior criminal record revealing a drug history, who admit use, or when other exigent circumstances indicate use.

Probation and parole agencies should establish an unscheduled urine specimen collection procedure that reduces opportunities for offenders to predict when specimens will be requested. Under most circumstances, casual or periodic drug use reduces the detection period because of the limited time most abused drugs remain in an individual's system. Frequent drug use increases the likelihood of detection. If urine specimens are collected on a predictable schedule, offenders will have the opportunity to discontinue their use long enough prior to urinalysis to avoid detection.

Initial drug tests (screens) should include a broad category of drugs (five or more drugs) to determine the offender's drug or drugs of choice. Once the drug(s) of choice has been determined, subsequent tests specific to these drug(s) can then be conducted. Periodically, a full screen should be ordered to determine if there is any change in drug(s) abused.

Confirmation Procedures

Confirmation tests are conducted to confirm initial drug test results and ensure that "false positive" results were not obtained. False positives occur when test results are positive, but drugs were not illicitly consumed. Results are based on comparisons with known specimens, and cutoff levels are used to determine whether the specimen is positive or negative. The cutoff level is the level of drug or drug metabolite that must be present in the specimen for the result to be reported as positive. For most confirmation tests, the cutoff level should be lower than the cutoff of the initial screening process. In the criminal justice setting, the use and acceptance of confirmation testing varies. Some courts accept results based on an initial test, a second test using the same or alternative methodology, or a written or signed admission from the offender. It is important that probation and parole agencies confirm which procedures the courts in their jurisdiction will accept.

The most recognized and supported confirmation procedure is Gas Chromatography/Mass Spectrometry (GC/MS). This procedure is capable of producing specific results. Probation and parole agencies should secure GC/MS confirmation for any drug testing program in which the results may warrant seeking revocation or other significant action against the offender.

Chain of Custody

One of the weakest elements of many drug testing programs is the lack of responsible specimen documentation. "Chain of custody" means accounting for the custody of the drug specimen from the time it is obtained from the offender up to and including the time the test results are presented as evidence in court. Following the proper chain-of-custody procedures can reduce errors and reinforce drug test results.

The chain-of-custody requirement ensures the specimen obtained from the offender is the same specimen that is tested. It further ensures that the results obtained from the test are the same results presented as evidence in court. Unless the proper chain of custody is maintained, the evidence is not admissible (technically) in court. The chain-of-custody document should contain at least the following:

- written receipt of the specimen (name, time, and date of each person having possession)

- information on the security of the specimen (e.g., location between receipt and final disposition)

- signature of the person responsible for attesting to the test's validity

- results of the test written on laboratory or agency letterhead

Reporting Results

Drug test results are often shared among probation, parole, and other affiliated agencies (e.g., treatment providers, courts, and parole boards). Details concerning who should be permitted access to test results, how they are to be shared, and where results are to be maintained should be clearly defined in agency drug testing policies and procedures. Agencies should develop strict controls that include how drug test results are to be transmitted and which agency personnel are authorized to receive them. Results should be returned by the test administrators to the designated agency in a timely manner. It is highly recommended that turnaround time be within forty-eight hours, seventy-two hours maximum. An extended lapse of time between specimen collection and test results may create unnecessary concern from offenders regarding the custodianship of their specimen and accuracy of the results.

Use of Results

Probation and parole agencies should establish policies and procedures on how drug test results should be used. For programs to effectively intervene and deter drug use, measures must be developed to hold offenders accountable for positive test results. Drug counseling and education offer offenders opportunities for rehabilitation that may ultimately divert or prevent them from continued drug use and criminal behavior.

Drug test results provide supervising officials valuable information regarding offender compliance or noncompliance with respect to supervision conditions. Results may be used to do the following:

- confront the offender

- hold the offender accountable

- determine most appropriate treatment modality

- impose increased sanctions

- seek modification or revocation action

It is important that some action be taken for every positive drug test result. Where permissible, agencies should establish a continuum of progressive sanctions to reinforce sobriety and abstinence. Accurate and consistent documentation procedures should be maintained on all drug test results and sanctions imposed. Sanctions short of incarceration may include the following:

- verbal and written reprimands

- increased testing frequency

- curfews

- increased office and field visits

- intensive supervision

- electronic monitoring

- outpatient or inpatient treatment

Determining which sanctions to use should depend on the number and frequency of positive results, periods of abstinence, the court's tolerance level, and agency policies. When a pattern of drug abstinence is established through negative drug test results, offenders should be rewarded with privileges that were not previously allowed.

Drug Testing as Part of a Treatment Program

Drug testing is not treatment. However, drug testing can be an exceptionally valuable part of a drug treatment program. Likewise, it can be counter-productive if it is not carefully administered. This also applies to drug testing programs operated by probation or parole agencies.

Drug testing, when incorporated with treatment, may be used as a diagnostic tool in screening and assessing offenders' drug involvement. It also serves as a means of monitoring offenders' compliance in remaining drug-free. The therapeutic value of drug testing, coupled with various treatment approaches, is difficult to evaluate. However, treatment programs that do not incorporate drug testing as part of their regimen have difficulty substantiating claims of success regarding program participants remaining drug-free.

When drug testing is used as part of a treatment program, drug test results must be handled carefully. Responding too quickly or punitively may be counter-therapeutic and may adversely affect a program's credibility. When programs are managed apart from probation and parole, steps should be taken to ensure fundamental data relative to the offender's progress are communicated between the treatment provider and the supervising probation or parole agency. Such interagency cooperation is very important. Probation and parole agencies should obtain written authorization from offenders for release of drug test results and other vital treatment information as appropriate to designated agencies.

Drug Testing Results in Violation and Revocation Hearings

The majority of courts in the United States has ruled that drug test results are admissible as evidence. Generally, there are four requirements for drug testing to be a valid condition of probation. It must be constitutional, clear, reasonable, and reasonably related to the protection of society and the rehabilitation of the individual (del Carmen & Sorensen 1988).

The use of drug testing in violation and revocation hearings generally requires the same amount of evidence as required in other legal proceedings. Most courts allow drug test results as evidence when assured that proper testing methodologies and procedures have been used. Likewise, requirements for confirming initial test results are not as strict as requirements for individuals who are not under probation or parole supervision (*Peranzo v. Coughlin*, 850 F2d 125 [CA2 1988]).

Considering the reliability and accuracy of most on-site drug testing methodologies available today and the established methodologies and practices of certified laboratories, drug test results used in violation and revocation hearings are rarely challenged. When challenges do arise, they usually concern chain-of-custody procedures, underscoring that proper chain-of-custody procedures are paramount to the integrity and credibility of drug testing programs. Drug test results may not be admissible as evidence unless chain-of-custody procedures are carefully followed.

Conclusion

There are many benefits to drug testing in probation and parole supervision. If the appropriate policies and procedures are put into place and followed, drug testing can be one of the best tools available for monitoring and controlling offender behavior. It can identify the drug-involved offender, help the offender admit to illicit drug use, serve as a deterrent, and aid the offender in getting treatment. Drug testing helps administrators develop supervision and case management plans concerning additional supervision or treatment strategies for offenders. Test results can also be used as evidence in court against the noncompliant offender.

Reference

del Carmen, R. V., and J. R. Sorensen. 1988. Legal issues in drug testing probationers and parolees. *Federal Probation* (December): 19–27.

9

Special Needs Offenders on Probation and Parole

By Annette Z. Henderson and Dee K. Bell

T he continued increase in the number of probation and parole caseloads has highlighted the complexity of problems that contribute to criminal behavior in society. Substance abuse, sex offenses, and violent offenses, including domestic cases, are some of the primary problems challenging society today. These multifaceted problems have received increased attention in recent years because of increasing societal awareness and intolerance of these problems, and its subsequent pressures for change. These demands have influenced legislation, sentencing patterns, and resource allocations. Research has also focused more specifically on identification issues and treatment interventions for various subpopulations.

Because handling special needs offenders on general caseloads, which are overloaded, has not sufficiently reduced or deterred criminal behavior, more sophisticated and specialized approaches for managing these offenders in the community have emerged in recent years.

This chapter will briefly outline guidelines for managing substance abusers, sex offenders, violent offenders, and offenders in domestic violence cases. These subcategories are not inclusive of all special needs popula-

tions; therefore basic case management principles applicable to any subpopulation are also discussed.

Results-oriented Supervision

Specific supervision strategies must be used for probation and parole supervision to deter and reduce criminal behavior in offender populations. Intervention, surveillance, and enforcement are necessary and complementary components of effective probation and parole supervision. Intervention strategies for special needs offenders must define specific behavioral and attitudinal changes that need to occur and services needed to assist these changes. These strategies should be clearly understood by officers and offenders and should be designed with a means to measure progress. Surveillance activities should support the intervention plan by monitoring for indicated risk and compliance with conditions.

The Broker: A New Role for Field Officers

Field officers are important links to the courts, human service programs, and the community. In the past, officers have attempted to meet offender needs on a one-to-one basis, but time and education specialization now limit this role. A new role as a broker is emerging for case management of offenders (Spica 1993).

Annette Z. Henderson, secretary for the American Probation and Parole Association, is assistant deputy commissioner Offender Services—Development for the Georgia Department of Corrections.

Dee K. Bell is Unit Director of Facility Support Services, Community Corrections, for the Georgia Department of Corrections.

As brokers, officers procure the needed treatment services indicated by the assessment of the special need offender. The officer's primary function in this role is to refer offenders to appropriate community program providers.

Spica (1993) outlines four assumptions that guide the referral process:

1. Offenders have needs that can best be met by human service providers.

2. Offenders can successfully change behavior on receipt of these services.

3. Use of human service specialists can enhance the capacity of offenders to change positively and allow officers time to devote to other duties.

4. Most services are not offered in the criminal justice system, but in the community social services network.

These assumptions apply to special needs offenders and the services they require. To be successful brokers for the offenders they supervise, officers must master case management skills and be very familiar with treatment programming options.

Case Management Skills

Case management is defined as a planned approach to offender management that is based on the needs, problems, capabilities, and limitations of offenders. Successful case management helps offenders change their behavior and become crime-free individuals. Case management is goal-driven, with the ultimate goal being a reduction in recidivism (APPA & NASADAD 1990).

There are five elements in successful case management: assessing, planning, linking, monitoring, and advocating.

Assessing

A thorough assessment process can effectively identify the needs of offenders and their risks to the community. Various types of assessments are used, depending on the offense type (e.g., substance abuser or sex offender). Assessment results can be used to make sentencing decisions and to influence necessary conditions of supervision, including treatment interventions.

Planning

Many field officers develop excellent planning skills from juggling the myriad demands made on their time. The planning involved in successful case management concerns developing a program plan that defines in writing the objectives of offender behavior change, the methods used to obtain the behavior change, and the standards of performance of the behavior change. The program plan emphasizes treatment services needed, criminal justice requirements or probation and parole conditions, and evaluation of the offender's progress. It provides field officers with a map for the supervision of individual offenders.

Linking

The third element of case management is linking the offender to the services specified in the program plan. Several types of services may be needed by special needs offenders. Treatment services are usually needed, but employment assistance, education or training programs, housing assistance, and medical services may also be required. For each service needed, the field officer serves as an important link between the offender and the service provider. The officer funnels necessary information to the service provider and receives information on the offender's progress. Relevant information needs to be shared with the treatment program or other providers while meeting confidentiality requirements.

A sure way to meet confidentiality requirements is to obtain written consent from the offender for information to be released to each treatment or service provider. When a written release is not obtained, the officer must adhere to confidentiality requirements regarding that specific situation.

The officer must match the offender's particular needs with the appropriate service provider. Key concepts in successful matches include the following:

1. Increased treatment. The length of treatment has been found to be associated with positive outcomes (Taxman 1991).

2. Treatment intensity. Offenders should be placed in the least restrictive setting that is appropriate to allow for individual accountability and adjustments if the initial placement is ineffective.

3. Mutual placement agreement. A placement that is supported by both the officer and the treatment provider has a greater chance for positive outcome. Offenders do not receive double messages and have

less room to maneuver between treatment personnel and the officer.

4. Offender motivating treatment. Studies have shown that offenders who are motivated to treatment or motivated by legal sanctions do equally well in treatment (Taxman 1991). The key to successful treatment is motivation by a consistent source, and often the officer can provide this motivation.

Monitoring

Monitoring is ascertaining the degree of compliance with the program plan achieved by the offender. Field officers should continuously observe offenders' progress and assess their success or failure so that success is reinforced and failure is sanctioned. Both success and failure lead to reassessment and changes in the offender's program plan.

The potential use of intermediate sanctions when there is a failure to progress should be discussed with offenders in advance. Offenders should know what to expect in response to specific behaviors. Many probation and parole agencies have developed a continuum of intermediate sanctions. These sanctions include increased urinalysis, community service hours, increased treatment, intensive probation or parole, short-term residential placement, and shock incarceration. When sanctions are used, it is important that the treatment providers involved are informed of the circumstances and the sanctions. This ensures a unified approach.

Field officers should be familiar with treatment options. Programs vary widely in differing localities, so each officer will have to invest some effort into locating available programs and assessing the program's success and suitability. When evaluating a program, the following areas should be considered (Spica 1993):

1. Has the provider worked well with offenders in the past?

2. What is the "success" rate of this program?

3. How does program cost compare with that of other programs?

4. Does the program share information with the supervising officer?

Advocating

The final case management element is advocacy. Advocacy is defined as interceding on behalf of the offender

to ensure appropriate services are provided (APPA & NASADAD 1990). There are two types of advocacy:

1. Case-specific advocacy ensures treatment services meet the individual's assessed needs.

2. Class-specific advocacy requires treatment providers to change to meet documented deficiencies in the treatment system.

In each case it is important that field officers advocate on behalf of offenders but remember that the protection of the public is part of the dual mission.

Intensive Supervision Programs

Intensive supervision programs (ISPs) are currently being used in many states to manage some special needs offenders, particularly sex offenders, violent offenders, and substance abusers. ISPs can be effective in reducing criminal behavior when they provide integrated approaches to controlling and assisting offenders. Studies have shown that ISPs should focus on intensive services because of the correlations between participation in treatment and recidivism (Fulton & Stone 1993). ISPs can provide strict monitoring in all environments encountered by offenders (work, home, school) through surveillance and emphasis on treatment options and compliance.

The close monitoring that is part of ISPs provides the control needed for offenders prone to violence. Many of these offenders have substance abuse problems that may lower their inhibitions and allow impulsive violent acts. ISPs can also be used to monitor offender compliance with court orders. Home visits by ISP officers may serve to deter violent offenders from acting out at home (Petersilia & Turner 1991). This combination of control and assistance to offenders is the goal of ISPs and makes them effective in managing the special needs offender.

Substance Abuse Programs for Community Supervision Offenders

The fastest growing offender population under community supervision is the substance abuser (Cunniff & Shilton 1991). The Drug Use Forecasting (DUF) system documents that drug users are involved in over 70 percent of all felony arrests in the twenty-two cities surveyed by

DUF in 1991. As the substance abusing offender population grows, field officers are mandated to become increasingly involved in brokering substance abuse treatment services for probationers and parolees. The critical factor in this mandate is that one-third of re-arrested offenders under community supervision was arrested for drug law violations (Cunniff & Shilton 1991). As community supervision systems struggle to provide community protection and offender rehabilitation to a fast-growing caseload, it is imperative that effective substance abuse programs be identified.

The Substance Abusing Offender

In criminal justice settings, the perspective for defining substance abusers has been the abuser's criminal history record. Although criminal history records are good indicators, studies have shown that many offenders arrested for crimes not related to drugs have serious drug abuse problems (National Institute of Corrections 1991). Profiles of drug-involved offenders may consider the following characteristics: financial status, employment status, education level, and self-perception. Personal characteristics, such as gender, race, age, and religious beliefs, are nonindicative.

One way to expand the profile of the drug-involved offender is to understand why people use and abuse drugs. There are three prominent categories of theories of substance abuse: biological, psychological, and sociological. One of the best known of the biological theories is the medical model of addiction. In brief, the medical model defines abuse and addiction as a disease that is biological and leads to pathological results.

A refinement of the medical model is the addictive disease model. This model defines addiction as a chronic, progressive, relapsing, incurable, and ultimately fatal disease caused by genetic abnormalities in the brain chemistry. It characterizes addictive disease symptoms as the compulsion to use drugs that leads to a loss of control of use despite the negative consequences to the individual.

Psychological theories of addiction and abuse focus on addictive behavior being promoted by the positive reinforcement of the pleasurable sensation of drug use, the negative reinforcement of feeling pain when not using, and the pathology of an inadequate or abnormal personality. Psychological theories explain substance abuse

Educating offenders on the dangers of drug abuse is an important part of many substance abuse programs. *(Officer standing.)*

as a response to emotional pain caused by low self-esteem or self-loathing attitudes.

Sociological theories of abuse and addiction seek to explain drug-involved behavior in terms of the abusing individual's relationship with society. These theories suggest the use is defined in progressive phases from experimentation to recreation to addiction. The progression from one phase to the next is supported by peer pressure, desire to take risk, and reinforcement of drug-involved behavior.

In reality, none of these theoretical models completely explains abuse and addiction. It is helpful for field supervision to define addiction as a bio-psycho-social dependence on any mood altering substance (Gorski & Miller 1986). The term "bio-psycho-social" recognizes that all areas of individual functioning are affected in abuse and addiction and that all areas must be addressed in recovery.

Abuse and addiction differ from simple use of a drug or alcohol by the lack of freedom of choice. Substance users decide when, where, and the quantity of use. Abusers and addicts are dictated the frequency, quantity, and nature of their use. All addicts begin with simple use, but not all use will lead to addiction.

Abusers experience a progression of symptoms often defined as stages. The early stage of addiction is characterized by a growing tolerance and dependence on the substance. The middle stage of addiction is primarily defined by an increasing loss of control in substance use.

Chronic stage addiction is signaled by the progressive deterioration of bio-psycho-social health. Offenders may be at any stage when they appear in the probation and parole system.

Supervision Methods for Drug-involved Offenders

Officers need special skills and resources to successfully manage drug-involved offenders. Specialized caseloads are a growing trend in handling special populations, and they are effective in managing drug abusers. The following are advantages of a substance abuse caseload:

- allows for specialized training in substance abuse for caseload officers

- encourages officers to build a strong network with local treatment and service providers

- emphasizes the offender remaining drug-free and compliant with treatment

Assessment

What are the determining factors for intervention? The method generally used in this determination is assessment of the offender's need for treatment and/or specialized supervision. Assessment may take into account several variables, and types of assessments vary from setting to setting. For field officers, the primary questions may be summed up as follows:

1. What are this offender's substance abuse activities?

2. Does the offender's substance abuse problem affect his or her likelihood of committing a new crime or successfully completing community supervision?

3. Is treatment appropriate for this offender?

One method of assessing offenders is to classify them by their commitment to crime and drug use. Offenders may be categorized in four classes: offenders with little commitment to crime and drugs are users, offenders committed to drugs but not to crime are addicts, drug-involved individuals committed to crime but not drugs are sellers, and offenders committed to both crime and drugs are predators.

These classes of drug offenders can then be referred to treatment services. Drug education or treatment should be directed toward users and addicts; control and monitoring programs should be used with sellers and predators (Taxman 1991). This perspective on assessment of drug-involved offenders is primarily a classification method because it looks at risk and need.

A more traditional assessment would seek to develop a holistic profile of offenders to determine their specialized needs. This approach seeks information in the following historical areas: drug, criminal, family, education, employment, treatment, and medical. Additional information may be sought in the areas of mental health status, motivation for treatment, and individual support system. This information is analyzed to determine supervision and treatment needs.

Assessment Tools

Several assessment tools are used in field supervision settings. All share the holistic approach of gathering data and then projecting the needed approach for offender treatment. Choosing one assessment tool can be a difficult task.

Assessment instruments fall into three major categories: copyrighted assessments, assessments designed by correctional agencies, and assessments developed by federal agencies. Copyrighted assessments, such as the Addiction Severity Index and Client Management Classification are valid, but generally have a fee associated with each use. Assessments designed by individual correctional agencies are generally developed for a specific program and may not have wide application. Often they have not yet been validated. Many are in the public domain. Federally developed instruments, such as the Drug Offender Profile Index, are in the public domain and are usually determined to be valid.

When selecting an assessment tool, it is helpful to remember that productive assessments must be able to determine the following (NIC 1991):

- the offender's drug use and current status

- the offender's criminal development

- the motivation of the offender for change

- the most appropriate treatment method

Case Management

Case management components, such as planning, linking, monitoring, and advocacy, described earlier are critical for effective management of this population. Case management ensures the offender's needs are met. If case management is too time consuming, outside agencies may be hired to provide these services.

Treatment Alternatives to Street Crime (TASC) agencies are such entities. TASC programs exist in many states and serve to link the criminal justice system with the treatment system. TASC programs provide all five elements of case management for offenders and facilitate communication between the field officer and the treatment provider.

Treatment Program Options

Drug Education Programs. Drug education programs are the least specific of all drug programs. Their primary purpose is to provide useful information on drugs and alcohol and their affect on individuals. Good programs seek to reduce denial in substance users.

Risk Reduction Programs. Risk reduction programs are targeted to alcohol using or abusing populations. These programs offer education and assist participants in making well-informed decisions regarding their use or nonuse of alcohol.

Group Treatment Programs. These programs combine a variety of treatment programs in the common modality of counselor-led peer group interactions. Groups may either be closed, having a consistent membership, or open, where members come and go at will. Studies have shown that both substance users and offenders respond well to peer-group interactions. It is helpful to have offenders contract to be involved in a group for a specific length of time because sporadic attendance decreases the potential for success.

Relapse Prevention Programs. Relapse prevention programs seek to help addicted offenders remain drug-free by teaching them the processes of recovery and relapse and how to recognize and successfully manage relapse warning signs. This program is most effective when conducted in a group setting.

Cognitive Restructuring Programs. Cognitive restructuring programs target the cognitive skill deficits found in most offenders. Cognitive skills training is based on the premise that offenders are undersocialized, and teaching values, reasoning, and social attitudes will assist offenders in modifying their impulsive, illogical, and egocentric behavior. These skills are also necessary in the recovery of substance abusers. Cognitive restructuring is primarily done in a group setting.

Twelve-step Programs. Twelve-step programs include Alcoholics Anonymous, Narcotics Anonymous, and Cocaine Anonymous. The purpose of twelve-step programs is to promote a sober and drug-free lifestyle by providing a fellowship of individuals who share their experiences to recover from a common addiction. These programs are for voluntary participants and have the advantage of being nationally available. Twelve-step programs are free, and their leaders will often work with field officers to ensure offender participation.

Sex Offenders

Managing sex offenders requires confronting sexuality. This problem is not caused by drugs, marital problems, or other stressors. It is about psychological problems expressed through distorted sexual practices. Most information on sex offenders pertains to male offenders, although there is some applicability to female offenders.

Sex offenders are paraphiliacs—individuals with a sustained deviant sexual interest. These offenders are usually grouped by offense type, such as child molesters, rapists, exhibitionists, voyeurs, etc. However, all of these offense types have similar characteristics and behavior patterns. "Current research indicates offenders are not necessarily limited to one type of deviant behavior but usually are involved in multi-deviant behavior patterns which expands the number of potential victims per offender" (Abel & Osborn 1992).

Sex offenders are very controlling and are skilled at manipulating, rationalizing, and lying. They deceive themselves and others about the devastating consequences of their actions. Sex offenders usually have a life-long history of faulty thinking and attitude and belief systems that are used to justify their pattern of sexual deviancy. "By relying on these distorted systems the sex offender is able to justify his/her actions and does not see themselves as the cause of any harm to the victims" (Abel & Osborn 1992).

Sex offenders use sexual aggression as a means to control their victims. Although sex offenses primarily revolve around issues of power and control, the role of the sex drive should not be underestimated. Generally, these offenders do not have problems with excessive sexual drive, but they often do have unusual paraphilia interests (Abel & Osborn 1992). Sexual orgasms are potent reinforcers of their deviant patterns of choice and cannot be easily substituted or changed. This is why treatment intervention is essential if behavior control and change is to occur.

No cure for these deviancies exist. Current studies of existing programs and treatment modalities indicate that recidivism rates can be reduced when certain key elements of assessment, supervision, intervention, and treatment strategies are applied. The following information is a summary of program components from sex offender programs in place around the country. This information is by no means all-inclusive, but it does provide some specific direction for those interested in establishing specialized caseloads for sex offenders under community supervision.

Assessment and Selection Process

Identification of an offender for placement in a sex offender program usually begins at the presentence stage. A thorough assessment process should be completed to guide sentencing decisions and establish the most appropriate supervision conditions and strategies for the offender. Ideally, all the following tools should be used to identify deviant behavior patterns and potential risk to the community:

- psychological testing

- two interviews by probation staff with the offender—one interview on social history and background and another interview on sexual history and background

- penile plethysmograph to identify and confront arousal patterns

- polygraph exam to improve validity of self-reported information

- probation staff interview with victim(s)

- risk assessment

McGrath (1992) points out that most corrections risk assessment instruments are of limited value in evaluating sex offenders because, except for their sexual offenses, most sex offenders have led stable and social lifestyles. McGrath describes five factors on which evaluators should focus their assessment of risk to better determine risk to the community:

1. What is the probability of reoffense? This requires identifying offense-type characteristics and the details associated with the offense to determine deviant behavioral patterns. Multiple convictions would indicate a higher risk than first-time convictions. During this phase, sex history information is obtained and may include the offender's knowledge of sex, range of sexual interests, and nature of deviant patterns. The

polygraph and penile plethysmograph can be used as tools to validate information. When inconsistences occur, behavior can be confronted and denial is reduced, contributing to a more effective treatment outcome.

2. What degree of harm is likely to result from reoffense? The best predictor of future violent behavior is past behavior, although if no history exists, it can't be ruled out. Masturbation fantasies should be investigated to determine whether they are sexually violent in nature as opposed to consensual. A plethysmograph can be used to help identify this propensity. The psychological damage to victims should also be taken into consideration.

3. Under which conditions is reoffense likely to occur? Penile plethysmography evaluations can determine variables that contribute to deviant behavior patterns. These variables include, but are not limited to, victim accessibility; alcohol and drug abuse, which are not causes but can disinhibit control; availability of pornography; negative emotional states (i.e., anger and depression); and idle-time activities.

   Probation and parole supervision and surveillance should be adjusted to monitor these specific variables to determine future deviant behavior.

4. Who would be the likely victims of a reoffense? Traditionally it has been thought that offenders who violate against one type of victim (e.g., a particular gender or age) in the past will reoffend the same type in the future. Current research indicates that most offenders engage in more than one category of deviant behavior and that a progression from hands-off offenses to hands-on offenses does occur. In addition, offenders may also have appropriate sex interests (Abel & Osborn 1992).

   Probation and parole officers need to be aware of all potential victims. Offenders with multiple sex deviancies present the greatest risk of reoffending. Plethysmograph results and inferences drawn from research about sexual deviant patterns can help with this assessment.

5. When is a reoffense most likely to occur? The patterns of sexually deviant behavior can be tracked to determine reoffense curves. Indicators, such as time of day, season of offense, and offender age, can be identified.

Supervision Conditions

For sex offenders, the conditions of supervision are very restricted and are aimed at identifying and controlling risk variables determined in the assessment process as reoffense indicators. For offenders to change their behavior, they must give up their need for control.

Treatment

Treatment for sex offenders is a long-term process. The treatment goal is to reduce or eliminate the offender's paraphiliac interest. Treatment confronts their distortions and blocks their ability to rationalize their behavior. Treatment modalities include covert sensitization, ammonia aversion, satiation, and overt behavior reversal. In general, they teach perpetrators the sequence of events leading to remission of the act and then provide specific information on how to disrupt the chain (Abel & Osborn 1992).

Cognitive-behavioral models are currently the most effective in reducing recidivism. The Relapse Prevention Model used in the Vermont Treatment Program for Sex Offenders is cognitively based and adaptable to the community setting. This intervention focuses on teaching offenders how to solve problems effectively and avoid putting themselves at risk for relapse.

Treatment is usually provided by local, public, or private mental health agencies or specialists. The relationship between the probation or parole officer and the counselor is very important. Each must attempt to understand the offender's deviant behavior patterns and support each other's efforts to confront inappropriate behavior and hold the offender accountable for progress.

Probation and Parole Intervention Programs

Where treatment resources for sex offenders do not exist in the community, field officers can attempt to block behavior by carefully monitoring conditions. They can advocate for treatment resources within the community and seek administrative support for obtaining specialized training, per diem consultant guidance in group structure, and other resources needed to run groups in-house.

Some probation departments have established sex offender intervention groups, where officers are involved in direct delivery of services, usually with the assistance of consulting psychologists or specialists. These groups are specific in nature, with objectives and measurable means to evaluate offenders' behavior.

Offenders placed with the Jefferson County, Missouri, sex offender program must progress through four levels of groups (Coxe & Hudgins 1992):

1. Denial group. The purpose of this level is to break through denial by having offenders describe the details of their offense, including thinking errors used to justify their acts, how they selected and groomed their victim, details of deviant actions, and how they controlled the victim and maintained secrecy.

2. Behavior group. This group uses various behavioral techniques to teach offenders how they can recognize and manage deviant arousal patterns.

3. Evening treatment group. The focus of this group is on relapse prevention, victim sensitivity, and learning and recognizing the deviant cycle.

4. Monthly evening groups (aftercare). It takes offenders two to three years to reach this level, and monthly follow-up supports previous group work for the duration of their supervision.

Selection Criteria for Officers to Work with Specialized Caseloads

Identifying individuals who can work effectively with sex offenders is difficult. Because of the highly emotional issues involved in managing these offenders it may be necessary to rotate staff periodically to avoid burn-out.

Officers should do the following (Scott 1992):

- volunteer due to interest

- be highly motivated

- be emotionally stable

- have a good sense of humor as a necessary healthy outlet

- have a willingness to be objective about issues that are emotionally charged

- have casework and family intervention skills

- have a sensitivity for victims' needs

Supervision Techniques

Stringent and restrictive techniques need to be applied to effectively monitor offenders' behavior and their environment for risk indicators. Surveillance techniques developed and used should also support intervention plans needed for their treatment progress. Supervision conditions and strategies help make offenders aware of shifts in personal control. This shift in power is often necessary before the offender will be motivated to change behavior. Consequently, supervision is a critical complementary component to treatment interventions. Where treatment sources are not available, effective supervision can still be an important part of preventing reoffenses.

The supervision and monitoring techniques used to manage sex offenders include assessment technologies previously discussed, as well as urinalysis testing, electronic monitoring, daily activity logs, curfew checks at high-risk times of day, family and employee interviews, and enrollment and participation in support groups.

Officers also need to be aware of the physical, psychological, and emotional trauma that occurs in victims. Victims can be revictimized, even if an actual reoffense does not occur. This psychological damage is particularly true in incest cases. Consequently, supervision should be focused not only on deterring future sexual abuse but also on preventing further psychological trauma to the victim (Abel & Osborn 1992).

Officers must also make clear to offenders that due to the nature of their offense they will not be trusted throughout their entire length of supervision. In addition, officers should stay current on research findings related to sex offenders so they can apply this knowledge to their assessment and supervision strategies (Scott 1992).

Supervision strategies in the Maricopa County program also suggest the following approaches (Scott 1992):

1. Schedule regular appointments to focus attention on the offender.

2. Communicate with the therapist involved to learn the offender's cycle of deviancy so the officer can talk to the offender about it and help him or her avoid it.

3. Ask the offender what he or she has learned in group session.

4. Monitor the offender's work, home, and spare-time activities.

5. Meet with the offender's spouse or significant others alone; be prepared for hostility.

6. Avoid religious counseling as primary treatment because well-meaning clergy often believe forgiveness and faith will fix the problem.

Holding offenders accountable for their actions is necessary for effective supervision outcomes. Consequently, officers need to develop a continuum of sanctions to be used when a violation occurs.

Officers should also use positive reinforcements when appropriate. Stringent conditions can always be modified based on the offender's progress. However, officers should keep in mind that these offenders are experts at manipulation, and that due to the nature of the offense the risk of relapse is high.

Training

Specialized training for officers and administrators on sex offender issues is necessary prior to beginning a program and is needed periodically after the program has begun. Training should consist of reviewing current research that identifies the profile of this population as well as interviewing, assessment, intervention/treatment, surveillance, and enforcement strategies.

Community Involvement

Sex offender issues have a direct relationship with social and community issues such as child abuse and domestic violence. Therefore a collaborative effort should be established within the community with other criminal justice entities, public and private corrections agencies, private businesses, and religious communities.

Violent Offenders

The supervision of violent offenders as a specialized population is a growing trend for probation and parole agencies. More information and research is needed to clearly define specific strategies for these offenders.

The Violent Offender Profile

Historically, violent offenders have been defined by their criminal history record. This is convenient in a criminal justice setting and may be sufficient to determine which offenders need specialized supervision. To better understand violent offenders it is helpful to look at their characteristics (Bolton & Bolton 1987; Vochelson & Samenow 1976):

• distorted cognition or thoughts

• egocentricity and shallow or distorted relationships with others

• inability to trust others or their motivations

Group counseling is often used to help offenders cope with their problems.

- low self-esteem (often linked to childhood abuse)

- less tolerance for stress and anxiety

- high need for control and dominance

- strong denial and defensiveness

- impulsive actions without thought or communication

- family history of violence

- inappropriate use of alcohol and/or drugs

- youthfulness or immaturity

On reviewing these characteristics, violent offenders look much like the rest of the offender population. Several of these characteristics point to the possible risk to society if these offenders do not learn to control their violence.

In supervising violent offenders, the successful merger of the dual mission of community protection and offender rehabilitation becomes critical. Field officers should control violent offenders through monitoring, while encouraging them to seek the necessary help to learn skills to control their violent behavior. One successful model for this is the brokerage model, which allows officers to serve as case managers for offenders and brokers for the most appropriate treatment from human service providers.

Several options for community supervision may be considered to provide for the close monitoring and control of violent offenders. Specialized caseloads are one option for supervision. Specialized caseloads of violent offenders should involve a small ratio of offenders to officers. Field officers supervising these offenders should clearly define the expectations and objectives of supervision. When compliance in actions and treatment is achieved, officers should praise offenders to reenforce the positive gain. Likewise, the offender must clearly understand the sanctions to be applied if the conditions of supervision are not met. This method of supervision requires probation and parole officers who are specially trained in techniques that control violence. These special officers are also involved in building networks with treatment service providers for violent offenders and in developing credibility with the courts as a supervisor of these high-risk offenders. Officers must always remember that community protection is the first priority in dealing with offenders with a propensity for violent behavior.

Programs to End Violent Behavior

In the 1970s, Yochelson and Samenow defined the criminal as incapable of functioning in society in a normal manner. In their definition, they found criminals operating in life with a pattern of automatic errors in thinking. As the errors compounded, the offender became stressed and angry. Those feelings, combined with low self-esteem, then erupted as violent behavior (Yochelson & Samenow 1976). To end the violence, this cycle of distorted cognition, rising frustration and anxiety, and acting out behavior must be interrupted. Field officers who manage violent offenders must be familiar with treatment programs designed to break this cycle.

Officers can evaluate local treatment programs by examining program components to see if they include those characteristics necessary for success with this population. Program characteristics include the following (Gondolf 1985):

- works with offenders to help them accept responsibility for their behavior

- breaks through the offenders' isolation

- develops strategies to reduce the offenders' stress and anxiety

- assists offenders in learning and using communication skills to express emotion

- teaches problem-solving and conflict-resolution skills

- builds offenders' self-esteem

- provides offenders with cognitive restructuring skills

These characteristics allow offenders to control their violent behavior and to deal with life in a positive manner. The following provides a general outline of treatment programs currently found to be successful with this population.

Aggression Replacement Training Programs

Aggression replacement training programs are offered in closed-group sessions with ten to twelve group members and a counselor or facilitator. These programs teach anger management skills, including identification of anger triggers, development of anger reducers, and breaking of anger cycles. The program then teaches cognitive skills and how to value others. The final stage of these programs teaches communication and problem-solving skills.

Relaxation Training Programs

Relaxation training programs seek to train violent offenders to interrupt the cycle by reducing stress, anxiety, and anger. Relaxation training teaches a variety of methods to achieve total relaxation in a matter of moments. This allows offenders to regain control of their thoughts and actions and not accelerate to violent behavior (Shelton & Levy 1981).

Cognitive Skills Training

Cognitive skills training programs seek to teach offenders techniques in problem solving, critical reasoning, values, creative thinking, social empathy, communication, and abstract reasoning. Studies by Ross and Fabriano have shown that cognitive restructuring increases offender self-esteem and decreases criminal behavior, including violence (Fogg 1992). Cognitive skills training has been used with incarcerated offenders in Canada since 1985. In 1991, the Colorado Judicial Department began a cognitive restructuring program for offenders under community supervision. More recently, programs have been started with probationers and/or parolees in Texas and Georgia (Fogg 1992).

Domestic Violence

Until recently, the problem of domestic violence has been largely ignored. According to Henson (1993), domestic violence happens "when one partner wants to control the other through fear and intimidation. It happens because there are so few negative consequences." This began to change as the criminal justice system and human service providers have begun to pay more attention to issues associated with domestic violence. As more and more domestic violence offenders enter the criminal justice system, probation and parole agencies have become more involved in managing these offenders and taking an active role in rehabilitation.

This section will discuss understanding the profile of the domestic violence offender, necessary treatment components, specialized training topics, and the necessity for interrogative intervention policies in dealing with this issue. Many case management principles and characteristics associated with violent and sex offenders also apply to this population.

Offender Profile

Domestic violence usually involves battery and stalking violations. Domestic violence is not caused by substance abuse, bad marriages, poor impulse control, or co-dependency. Domestic violence is about coercive control patterns of violence. These offenders are manipulative and have a strong sense of entitlement. They are often psychologically abusive to their victim prior to the onset of physical violence. They may have unrealistic rules and conditions with which they insist their victims comply. If compliance is not forthcoming, the offender feels justified in abusing the victim. In this respect, these violent responses are often premeditated. The offender's private behavior may be very different from his or her public image, which is often very charming and social in nature (Buel 1993).

Probation and Parole Programs

Probation and parole officers usually become involved with domestic violence cases when restraining orders have been violated. The officer's primary responsibility is the safety of the victim. Probation and parole supervision holds the offender accountable for his or her actions by monitoring compliance with court-ordered conditions and by working closely with treatment providers.

Assessment

Agencies should conduct a thorough assessment to determine offender suitability for placement in an in-house program or referral to treatment programs. The assessment may include interviews with the offender, an interview with the victim, a social and criminal background history interview, determination of the offender's denial status, and any needed psychological testing. Offenders currently on medication should be referred to a human service provider to assess treatment needs. Psychopathic or sociopathic offenders should'nt be placed in in-house programs.

Some probation and parole agencies have established domestic violence groups. These groups are usually psychoeducational in nature and the curriculum consists of values clarification, anger management, communication skills, and sensitivity training.

Some offenders who are determined inappropriate for group participation may be seen individually by a specially trained officer or a counselor. However, most agencies will refer such an individual to a human service provider for treatment. Research indicates that many successful domestic violence offender programs have the following components (Buel 1993):

1. Treatment is court-ordered, with probation and parole officers enforcing this condition.

2. Programs are at least one year long.

3. Programs are based on the cognitive-behavioral concept.

4. Participation is voluntary.

Interacting with Victims of Domestic Violence

Community supervisors and administrators should have specialized training in domestic violence issues. This will help them determine the best approaches and intervention for their system. Probation and parole officers should be taught not to blame victims and to recognize and understand the obstacles to learning that may limit the offender's progress.

Officers should also be trained in understanding the victim's point of view. Leaving the abusive environment doesn't ensure the victim's safety and may, in fact, be dangerous. The following are some reasons victims remain in abusive situations:

- financial security
- children
- fear
- guilt
- shame
- ignorance of options
- societal pressure
- family pressures
- self-denial
- religious beliefs
- lack of mobility
- hope that things will change
- lack of job skills
- fear of physical isolation
- low self-esteem

In interviewing victims and attempting to identify past and current abuse, the following five statements may help officers establish an environment of trust and openness (Buel 1993):

1. I'm afraid for your safety (which helps combat self-minimalization).

2. I'm afraid for the safety of your children.

3. The situation will only get worse without intervention.

4. I'm here for you when you are ready.

5. You deserve better than this, and I can assist you in contacting the police or a local shelter for abuse victims.

It is important that a safety plan for victims be developed. The safety plan would help victims prepare the following information to ensure safety whenever he or she decides to leave. The plan should include the following (Buel 1993):

- a list of friends, family, and shelters that can help

- a list of essentials, such as checkbook, birth certificate, etc.

- a plan to confide in someone at work, home, school, etc., about the existence of a restraining order

- an alternative plan in case the shelters are full

Summary on Domestic Violence Offenders

Research indicates that a direct relationship exists among child abuse, domestic violence, and juvenile delinquency. Because of the complex nature of these issues, collaborative efforts should be made with representatives from the District Attorney's Office and the courts, legislators, corrections personnel, probation and parole staff, human service providers, educators, medical professionals, and private businesses to develop coordinated and integrated responses to these problems. These efforts should include educating the community about the domestic violence problem and eliciting community support in helping to inform victims about assistance programs.

Conclusion

The number of offenders with special needs will continue to increase. Probation and parole systems must adapt their practices to more effectively manage these offenders if long-term behavior change and reduction in recidivism is to occur. This will require continually challenging the probation and parole professional and individual systems to strive for and develop, implement, and evaluate supervision strategies. These strategies must become more specific in defining the most effective balance among intervention, surveillance, and enforcement and the desired outcomes for these special needs populations.

Obtaining support for specialized approaches is difficult because of limited resources and competing priorities within the criminal justice system. However, applying the case management principles outlined in this chapter—assessing, planning, linking, monitoring, and advocating to high-need caseloads—provides a framework from which to build. It is through local community collaboration with other vested stakeholders that needed changes will occur in probation and parole practices, which will ultimately affect long-term behavioral change (reduced recidivism) in offenders.

References

Abel, G. G., and C. Osborn. 1992. Stopping sexual violence. *Psychiatric Annals* (June): 301–306.

American Probation and Parole Association and the National Association of State Alcohol and Drug Abuse Directors. 1990. *Interagency drug project training curriculum.* Lexington, Ky.: American Probation and Parole Association.

Bolton, F. G., and S. R. Bolton. 1987. *Working with violent families: A guide for clinical and legal practitioners.* Newbury Park, Calif.: Sage Publications.

Buel, S. M. 1993. *State-of-the-art-interventions in family violence: What works.* Presentation at the Community Corrections Saving Dollars and Lives Symposium. Tampa, Fl., 24 May.

Bureau of Justice Assistance. 1988. *Treatment alternatives to street crime (TASC): Training manual.* Washington, D.C.: Bureau of Justice Assistance.

Coxe, R., and F. Hudgins. 1992. An evaluation of a community-based sex offender program. *Perspectives* (Fall): 30–37.

Cuniff, M. A., and M. K. Shilton. 1991. *Variations on felony probations persons under supervision in 32 urban and suburban counties.* Washington, D.C.: National Association of Criminal Justice Planners.

Fogg. V. 1992. Implementation of a cognitive skills development program. *Perspectives* (Winter): 24–26.

Fulton, B., and S. Stone. 1993. The promise of new ISP. *Perspectives* (Winter): 43–45.

Gondolf, E. W. 1985. *Men who batter*. Holmes Beach, Calif.: Learning Publications.

Gorski, T. T., and M. Miller. 1986. *Staying sober: A guide for relapse prevention*. Independence, Mo.: Herald Housel Independence Press.

Henson, M. 1993. Vows of violence. *State Government News* (March).

McGrath, R. J. 1992. Five critical questions: Assessing sex offender risk. *Perspectives* (Summer): 6–10.

National Institute of Corrections. 1991. *Intervening with substance abusing offenders: A framework of action*. Washington, D.C.: National Task Force on Correctional Substance Abuse Strategies.

Petersilia, J., and S. Turner. 1991. Is ISP a viable sanction for high risk probationers? *Perspectives* (Summer): 8–11.

Scott, L. 1992. Maricopa County comprehensive sex offender treatment program. *Executive Exchange*: 2–5.

Shelton, J. L., and R. L. Levy, eds. 1981. *Behavioral assignments and treatment compliance: A handbook of clinical strategies*. Champaign, Ill.: Research Press.

Spica, R. 1993. What is between human services and offender adjustment? *Perspectives* (Winter): 24–26.

Taxman, F. S. 1991. Substance abuse treatment within the criminal justice system: An analysis of conflicting needs and implications. *Perspectives* (Summer): 18–26.

Yochelson, S., and S. E. Samenow. 1976. *The criminal personality: A profile for change*. New York: Jason Aronson.

APPLICABLE ACA STANDARDS

Standards for Adult Probation and Parole Field Services
Administration, Organization, and Management 2-3011, 2-3013, 2-3022
Fiscal Management 2-3084
Supervision—Probation and Parole Agencies 2-3105, 2-3110, 2-3111, 2-3116, 2-3122, 2-3129, 2-3131 to 2-3135
Supervision—Parole Agencies Only 2-3172, 2-3177

10

Probation and Parole and the Community

By Dan Richard Beto and Arlene Parchman

For probation and parole agencies to successfully address the needs of offenders and their communities, agency administrators need to develop cooperative partnerships with individuals and organizations that deliver human services. This has become particularly true during the past two decades when community corrections agencies—many operating under fiscal constraints—have been asked to take on an increasing number of high-risk and needy offenders because of crowded prisons and jails. The severity of problems presented by these offenders means additional administrative duties are necessary to provide enhanced services with limited financial resources. In the face of staff and agency limitations, many community corrections administrators have adopted a number of strategies to provide needed services (Beto 1987).

The following are some examples of successful approaches to these problems (Jensen 1987; Nelson, Segal & Harlow 1984; Shields, Chapman & Wingard 1983):

Dan Richard Beto is the director of the Judicial District Community Supervision and Corrections Department for Crimes, Madison and Walker Counties, headquartered in Huntsville, Texas.

Arlene Parchman is the director of the Brazos County Community Supervision and Corrections Department in Bryan, Texas.

A portion of this chapter originally appeared in the Coordinated Interagency Drug Training Project: Participant Manual (released in 1991) by the American Probation and Parole Association and the National Association of State Alcohol and Drug Abuse Directors through a grant from the Bureau of Justice Assistance.

- enhanced staff training in specialized areas

- development or expansion of in-house programs or initiatives to address the needs of a particular category of offender

- improved interagency cooperation in serving common clients

- negotiation of interagency agreements or contracts for specific services

- use of volunteers to assist in achieving the agency's objectives

These strategies have proven successful and have subsequently received wide acceptance. This chapter will focus on community corrections and its interorganizational role with other human service agencies, contracting for special services, and the use of volunteers.

Interorganizational Relationships and Contracting for Services

"Interorganizational relationships" is the term used to describe interagency partnerships. These relationships are defined as the "variety of interactions between two or more organizations designed to enhance organizational goals" (Hasenfeld & English 1983). Interorganizational relationships stem from each organization's ideal need for elements to reach its goals. These elements may be consumers, labor services, or other resources. The scarcity of elements leads to a restriction of the community corrections agency's activities as they relate to specific functions. To expand on the limited functions or resources and to benefit offenders served, exchanges should be made with other organizations and agencies in the community. These exchanges may be of varying proportions and are defined as "any voluntary activity between two organizations which has consequences, actual or anticipated, for the realization of their respective goals or objectives" (Levine & White 1983).

For offenders under noncustodial supervision to receive maximum benefit from available social services and community resources, community corrections personnel must cultivate positive working relationships with other human service agencies. These agencies and resources may include any of the following:

- mental health centers that offer psychological, psychiatric, substance abuse, and mental retardation services

- substance abuse education and counseling, as well as family counseling

- educational and vocational services that offer adult basic education services, preparation and acquisition of a high school equivalency certificate, and vocational testing and training

- human resource or welfare agencies that provide child or elderly abuse services, family counseling, monthly income for low-income families, food stamps, and other specialized programs (Walsh 1992)

- residential facilities that provide treatment to address the needs of a particular type of client or problem

- agencies assisting with food and shelter in emergencies, as well as assisting with housing needs and meeting other financial needs in times of crisis

- organizations addressing the needs of the handicapped

- health services, such as basic medical and dental care

- employment services agencies

- support groups

Agencies and organizations that provide these services are important components of the criminal justice system. Community corrections professionals as "brokers of services" should familiarize themselves with the services of these agencies and their eligibility criteria. As brokers of services, community corrections professionals make many referrals for services as an adjunct to providing basic supervision. Critical to this process is the appropriateness of the referral. Prior to making any referral, community corrections administrators should conduct a needs assessment to determine those areas where offenders require

Officers should be aware of community services groups, such as Goodwill Industries, that offer vocational training and other services.

assistance to encourage positive social lifestyles, promote a conflict-free period of supervision, and place those under supervision in a more advantageous position to compete in a complex society.

To make appropriate referrals for services, officers should develop and frequently update a resource manual that describes each organization and agency serving the area, including contact person's name, hours of operation, eligibility criteria, services available, cost of services, and the agency's address and phone number. As needs are identified among offenders, referrals can be done quickly and efficiently through a well-maintained resource manual.

If a resource manual has not been developed, senior officers and supervisory personnel should be consulted about available services. These individuals should be able to direct officers to the appropriate personnel in the various agencies and organizations who are available to answer questions and who can provide current literature on services offered. Files should be developed with pertinent information for offenders categorized by type of agency for quick reference.

Interorganizational resources are best developed and maintained through personal contact and are most effective when formalized through joint-purpose statements, interagency agreements, and contracts for services.

Formalized agreements should be made only after a needs assessment is conducted. A formal needs assessment consists of the following:

- define initial goals and objectives

- determine questions to be addressed

- identify relevant participants

- review existing data

- select data collection techniques

- collect data

- analyze and interpret data

- redefine goals and objectives

- determine priorities

- communicate the needs assessment findings to decision makers and staff

The results of the needs assessment may suggest any of the following service delivery options (Reid 1964; Jensen 1987):

- operating a program in-house

- entering into a joint-purpose statement

- issuing vouchers, thus enabling eligible offenders to obtain services from single or multiple vendors

- entering into a cooperative agreement with an organization to better serve common clients

- contracting with "for profit" organizations or professionals

- contracting with voluntary, nonprofit, or tax-supported organizations

The ultimate decision on the strategy selected should be based on a careful analysis of the following factors: (1) cost effectiveness, (2) quality of service, (3) ease in service delivery, and (4) the willingness of the political environment to support the decision (Florestano & Gordon 1980; Jensen 1987; Paulson 1988; Nessen 1990).

Joint-purpose Statements

Joint-purpose statements are tools through which two or more organizations acknowledge why they should come together to work as partners on a common problem. The statement identifies the problem to be addressed, outlines the interest the agencies have in working together, and establishes what each agency can contribute to the concerted effort.

A joint-purpose statement acknowledges that the agencies have a vested interest in working cooperatively, the two agencies have a common clientele, and both agencies provide services that contribute to the management of the targeted offender.

The joint-purpose statement is a vehicle through which agencies can identify common problems and clients. The statements do not, for the most part, actually commit either agency to any particular course of action. They can, however, prepare a framework that may eventually develop into an interagency agreement.

Interagency Agreements

An interagency agreement is a formal means of solidifying cooperation between agencies. Interagency agreements are designed to clarify tasks, roles, and responsibilities of each agency. The more specific the agreement, the fewer problems are encountered in the relationship between agencies.

A number of issues should be covered in interagency agreements. These issues include the following:

- treatment services provided

- notification and discharge communication

- treatment and referral criteria

- confidentiality issues

- frequency and type of offender contact

- assessment criteria

- frequency and type of contact between agencies

- success and failure criteria

- provisions for periodic review and modification

- other factors relevant to the service of common clients

Interagency agreements provide two levels of satisfaction for agencies. For administrative staff, the agreements provide formalized interagency cooperation. For line staff, the agreements provide a guide to activities relating to other agencies.

Contracts

Some interagency agreements may call for remuneration for services rendered. These agreements then become contracts for services. Contracts for services should be structured to include formalization, intensity, reciprocity, and standardization.

Formalization refers to "the degree to which exchanges between organizations are given official sanction and are agreed to by the parties involved and the extent to which an intermediary coordinates the relations" (Duffee 1980a). The formalization of a contract occurs when the contract becomes a written document, is approved by the appropriate administrator, and is handled by an appointed person or agency division.

Intensity involves the relationship between the frequency of interaction and the size of the resource invested (Duffee 1980a). The higher the resource invested, the more frequent the interaction should be.

Reciprocity involves who is receiving services, who is receiving remuneration, and the extent to which terms of the exchange are mutually reached (Duffee 1980a).

Standardization refers to the reliable determination "of the units of exchange and procedures for exchange between the organizations" (Duffee 1980a).

By formalizing the contract and ensuring that it includes the elements of intensity, reciprocity, and standardization, few problems should occur during the contractual period.

Potential contract services include the following (Beto 1987):

- psychiatric services, including examinations and evaluations, counseling, medication, and treatment

- psychological services, including evaluations, individual counseling, general group counseling, and specific group counseling for substance abusers, sex offenders, family dysfunction, and assaultive behavior

- medical facilities, including psychiatric, crisis intervention, detoxification, urinalysis, aftercare, and physical examinations

- residential facilities, including basic housing and emergency shelter, mental health and mental retardation centers, and substance abuse facilities

- general counseling

- substance abuse treatment

- vocational training

- preparation for a high school equivalency certificate

- literacy skills

- general life skills

- intermediate sanction facilities or other intermediate sanction options

- contracts with schools and institutions of higher learning for psychological services, special needs programs, and educational programs

Most contracts contain similar primary and secondary elements (Scherman 1987; Marlin 1984). Primary elements include the following:

- an opening paragraph

- the scope of the contract

- compensation for services and how payment will be made

- affirmative action

- confidentiality issues

- cancellation or modification procedures

- the contract period

The secondary elements include the following:

- provisions for extensions

- indemnity

- insurance

- bonding

- independent contractor status

- audits

- reports and monitoring procedures

- incorporation status

- whether there can be an assignment of responsibilities to another agency

Formalizing relationships between community corrections agencies and those agencies and organizations that deliver human services develops mutual support. This, in turn, promotes cohesiveness and efficiency in addressing the needs of a troubled population (Duffee 1980b).

Volunteers in Community Corrections

According to Terrell (1979), "There has been an upsurge of interest in contracting as a method of delivering human services, especially at the local government level." This assessment is supported by a review of current correctional practices that reveals community corrections agencies, in varying degrees, enter into formal relationships and contract for a number of services for offenders. Just as there has been an upsurge of interest in developing interorganizational relations, so too has there been an increase in the use of volunteers to deliver services to offenders (Scheier 1970; Kratcoski 1982; Sigler & Leenhouts 1982). This increased interest in volunteers is based in part on increased fiscal constraints and the realization of the importance of the volunteer in the criminal justice system (Smith 1992).

Volunteer programs in community corrections should be designed to enhance and promote the goals of the agen-

cy and should complement and supplement services offered by community corrections personnel. Volunteer programs should begin with an effective planning process, which includes a needs assessment of both the agency and the offender population. Goals and objectives should be determined, job descriptions written, and staff should be committed to the program. Volunteer programs function best when they are formalized and a coordinator is in place.

Once this is done, all staff should be oriented to the program, and community resources and recruiting methods should be determined. An effective volunteer program represents a partnership with the community, in which the community accepts the importance of the program and believes in its effectiveness (National Council of Jewish Women 1975). Volunteers should be screened and trained. The volunteer's skills should be matched with the appropriate job to maximize the use of skills (Unkovic & Davis 1969). Ongoing records of the program should be maintained, and staff, offenders, and volunteers should be allowed to evaluate the program on a regular basis.

The effectiveness of a volunteer program rests in the ongoing maintenance and development of the program. New volunteers must be continually recruited, selected, and oriented. Training must be continual, and volunteers must be motivated and recognized by program staff (Texas Department of Human Resources Volunteer Services 1983).

Volunteers make their time available for a number of reasons that range from idealistic to self-serving (Hunter 1984). Knowing the motivation behind an individual's desire to volunteer can help the community corrections administrator determine the best job in which to place the volunteer. Volunteers may be used in a number of positions, from clerical work to work as paraprofessionals in helping officers with their casework. Volunteers may serve as tutors, counselors, teachers, life skills educators, mentors, role models, substance abuse educators, employment coordinators, and volunteer coordinators. They may also be used in fund raisers, public relations initiatives, legal assistance, and specific technical areas. Volunteers may serve on advisory committees. This service, if clearly defined and meaningful, can promote the goals and objectives of the community corrections agency in the community.

A sound volunteer program can help free officers from some duties so that they are better able to identify problem areas, maintain supervision of probationers and parolees, and provide additional services not normally available to offenders. Volunteers who develop a sense of ownership in the organization serve an effective public relations function and can promote the agency's initiatives in the community.

Conclusion

Cooperative relationships between community corrections agencies and organizations that deliver human services are critical to realizing the goals of an overburdened criminal justice system. With this in mind, the use of area resources and the development and maintenance of interorganizational relations, both formally and informally, should be fully exploited by community corrections administrators and staff. Likewise, the creation of a meaningful volunteer program within the agency will not only assist in better serving the offender population but will also engender community support for and satisfaction with the community corrections agency and the criminal justice system.

References

Beto, D. R. 1987. Contracting for services. *Texas Probation* 2 (July): 9–10.

Duffee, D. 1980a. *Correctional management: Change and control in correctional organizations.* Englewood Cliffs, N.J.: Prentice-Hall.

——. 1980b. *Explaining criminal justice.* Cambridge, Mass.: Oelgeschlager, Gunn and Hain.

Florestano, P. S., and S. B. Gordon. 1980. Public v. private: Small government contracting with the private sector. *Public Administration Review* 40 (January-February): 29–34.

Hasenfeld, Y., and R. A. English. 1983. Interorganizational relations. In *Human service organizations: A book of readings,* ed. Y. Hasenfeld and R. A. English, 540–44. Ann Arbor, Mich.: University of Michigan Press.

Jensen, C., ed. 1987. *Contracting for community corrections services.* Washington, D.C.: National Institute of Corrections.

Levine, S., and P. E. White. 1983. Exchange as a conceptual framework for the study of interorganizational relationships. In *Human service organizations: A book of readings,* ed. Y. Hasenfeld and R. A. English, 545–60. Ann Arbor, Mich.: University of Michigan Press.

Kratcoski, P. C. 1982. Volunteers in corrections: Do they make a meaningful contribution? *Federal Probation* 46 (June): 30–35.

Marlin, J. T., ed. 1984. *Contracting municipal services: A guide for purchase from the private sector.* New York: John Wiley and Sons.

National Council of Jewish Women. 1975. Volunteers interact with the juvenile justice system. *Federal Probation* 39 (March): 39–41.

Nelson, E. K., L. Segal, and N. Harlow. 1984. *Probation under fiscal constraints.* Washington, D.C.: National Institute of Justice.

Nessen, P. 1990. The business of human services. *IARCA Journal* 3 (September).

Paulson, R. I. 1988. People and garbage are not the same: Issues in contracting for public mental health services. *Community Mental Health Journal* 24 (Summer): 91–102.

Reid, W. 1964. Interagency coordination in delinquency prevention and control. *Social Service Review* 38 (March).

Scheier, I. H. 1970. The professional and the volunteer in probation: Perspectives on an emerging relationship. *Federal Probation* 34 (June): 12–18.

Scherman, R. 1987. Contract development. In *Contracting for community corrections services,* ed. C. Jensen. Washington, D.C.: National Institute of Corrections.

Shields, P. M., C. W. Chapman, and D. R. Wingard. 1983. Using volunteers in adult probation. *Federal Probation* 47 (June): 57–64.

Sigler, R. T., and K. J. Leenhouts. 1982. Volunteers in criminal justice: How effective? *Federal Probation* 46 (June): 25–29.

Smith, J. S. 1992. Corrections' untapped resources: The community's volunteers. In *Juvenile careworker resource guide,* 108–12. Laurel, Md.: American Correctional Association.

Terrell, P. 1979. Private alternatives to public human services administration. *Social Service Review* 53 (March): 56–74.

Texas Department of Human Resources Volunteer Services. 1983. *Volunteer services guidebook: For administrators only.* Austin, Tex.: Texas Department of Human Resources.

Unkovic, C. E., and J. R. Davis. 1969. Volunteers in probation and parole. *Federal Probation* 33 (December): 41–45.

Walsh, A. 1992. *Correctional assessment, casework & counseling.* Laurel, Md.: American Correctional Association.

APPLICABLE ACA STANDARDS

Standards for Adult Probation and Parole Field Services
Administration, Organization, and Management 2-3008, 2-3011, 2-3012
Fiscal Management 2-3084
Management Information and Research 2-3090, 2-3095
Supervision—Probation and Parole Agencies 2-3127, 2-3129 to 2-3136
Citizen Involvement and Volunteers 2-3202 to 2-3206

11

Victims

By Linda F. Frank, Mario A. Paparozzi, and Brett M. Macgargle

Probation and parole professionals represent one of the few components of the criminal justice system that is community-based. These professionals are the eyes and ears of the courts and parole boards. It is appropriate for probation and parole agencies to provide services to victims after the criminal case has been adjudicated. Many victims contend that the trial and sentencing phases alone do not bring closure to the pain and suffering caused by the offender. Victims argue that as long as offenders are involved in any aspect of the criminal justice process, then the victims, too, are involved. In the past, and in many current cases, victims have been shut out of the justice process once the adjudication phase has been completed.

Increasingly, courts and parole boards are recognizing the need to address victims' concerns in the probation and parole phases. As a direct result of the work of certain victims' groups, the criminal justice system has been pressured to include victims in its processes. Many victims' groups have served to raise the level of consciousness of the public and of criminal justice administrators.

When working with victims, either individually or in groups, probation and parole agencies are in a good position to develop constructive relationships and to promote probation and parole services by articulating the tangible results of community supervision.

Linda F. Frank is a former victim services specialist for the American Probation and Parole Association in Lexington, Kentucky.

Mario A. Paparozzi is assistant chief for the New Jersey Bureau of Parole.

Brett M. Macgargle is director of Victim Services for the South Carolina Department of Probation, Parole, and Pardon Services.

Probation and parole professionals should work to increase the public's awareness of their role by addressing the concerns of crime victims.

One way to do this is through meetings with those concerned about victims' rights. This type of interaction between community corrections practitioners and victims helps victims to become more aware of the everyday process of supervision and helps probation and parole staff to become more sensitive to the concerns of victims. Increasing public awareness about the practice of probation and parole requires that the probation and parole system be in a position to clearly state its objectives and its success or failure in achieving accountability.

Victims of crimes, through no fault or cause of their own, suffer physically, emotionally, and financially. In addition, the families and friends of crime victims are also affected by the criminal act. Most victims, especially those who were victims of violent crimes, feel their lives and the lives of their families and friends have been irrevocably changed.

Although significant strides have been made in sensitizing various components of the criminal justice system to the needs and rights of victims, this process is not complete. In fact, the process of defining victims' rights is as open-ended as the process that has defined the rights of offenders since the inception of criminal and case law in America.

Secondary victimization occurs when victims are deprived of participating in the criminal justice process because certain fundamental rights of victims are violated. Given efforts to include victims in the criminal justice process at the arrest and prosecutorial stages, other stages of the criminal justice process should follow suit. Probation and parole are components of the criminal justice system that victims must interact with to complete the circle of their involvement in a case. Incorporating comprehensive victim services into probation and parole settings will minimize secondary victimization.

Victims' Bill of Rights

Victims have coordinated their efforts through several private, nonprofit associations to develop and incorporate into law a Victims' Bill of Rights. The Bill of Rights covers several major concerns of victims, including the following:

- the right to be informed

- the right to be kept advised of case progress

- the right to be treated with dignity

- the right to be made whole again

If probation and parole agencies do not actively participate in the development of victim-sensitive programming, a major portion of the criminal justice system will not be in a position to comply with the spirit and intent of the law. Incorporation of victim services into probation and parole settings provides a clear endorsement of the Victims' Bill of Rights.

Victims have argued for, and won, the right to be kept informed of the status of cases in which they are involved. Probation and parole are continuations of the criminal justice processing of a case. Keeping victims informed as to supervision status of the offender, offender adjustment in the community, offender ability to pay restitution, and geographical area of an offender's supervision are all logical extensions of the victim's right to be informed. Probation and parole agencies need to develop mechanisms to exchange information with victims in a timely and consistent manner.

Similarly, victims have established their right to be present and heard during the prosecutorial and sentencing phases of a criminal case. Therefore, victims should be afforded the opportunity to be present and heard at preliminary and final revocation hearings in the probation and parole process.

Restitution plays a key role in the victim's right to be made whole. Restitution is one tangible way victims can feel they are given something back that was taken from them. Although restitution can never undo the damage

done by the criminal act, it does in some small way facilitate the journey to wholeness.

Victim Impact Statements

Victim impact statements are critical components of the criminal justice process because the American system of justice considers a crime an act committed against society. Victims have historically been viewed as mere witnesses, complainants, or even evidence in criminal trials. One of the major successes of the nation's victims' rights movement has been to substantially alter such views and to make the victim an integral part of key decision making in criminal prosecutions. Nowhere is this success more evident than in the implementation of victim impact statements.

Victim impact statements are important for the following reasons:

1. Victims are given the opportunity to tell the court how the defendant's criminal act has detrimentally affected their lives.

2. The financial, emotional, physical, and psychological effects crime has on victims should be considered in determining a fair and appropriate sentence.

3. A victim impact statement can help the court determine appropriate restitution orders to fully compensate victims for expenses resulting from the crimes committed against them.

Procedures, protocols, and the victim impact statement forms themselves vary according to the jurisdiction, agency, or personnel involved in victim services. However, efforts are now being made to standardize the process to serve crime victims.

Victim impact statements should be included in the files of convicted offenders sentenced to prison. These statements can then be referred to prior to parole hearings. Parole officials should contact victims prior to parole hearings and provide them with an opportunity to update their victim impact statement or submit a new victim impact statement. Often, the long-term effects of a crime will differ from the information included in the victim's initial statement, and it is important that the parole authority have such information prior to making its decision.

Often, probation officers' assessment of the effect of crime on victims is based solely on information received from the prosecutor or law enforcement agencies.

Although such information is important, in many cases it is incomplete. Probation officers should initiate direct contact with victims, in person, by telephone, or in writing to receive pertinent feedback.

Keeping Victims in the Loop

Many victims feel that the postsentencing phases of their cases constitute a black hole in terms of the dissemination of information relevant to their cases. A coalition of criminal justice and victim service agencies in applicable jurisdictions (federal, state, and local) should establish clearly defined, written policies and procedures for notifying victims about offenders' status, including the following:

- sentencing

- incidence of absconding from probation or parole supervision

- probation or parole violation and related hearings

- probation or parole revocation and related hearings

- release from probation or parole supervision

Victims should be given the opportunity to do the following:

- submit (or resubmit) a victim impact statement, when applicable

- submit special requests as to when or where the offender can be released

- submit requests for no contact between the offender and the victim or his or her family members

- submit other relevant information pertinent to their cases

Many jurisdictions have created community or institutional advisory boards to help professionals in law enforcement, criminal justice, and institutional and community corrections. These advisory boards review requirements, policies, and procedures relevant to victim participation and revise such standards as needed. These programs ensure the victim is heard throughout all stages of the criminal justice and corrections processes.

Community or agency boards should involve representatives from the sponsoring agency, victim service agencies, victim support groups (victims themselves), and groups (such as the Salvation Army and Volunteers of America) that assist offenders and former offenders. These boards should meet at least twice a year.

Incorporating Victim Services into the Scope of Probation and Parole Responsibilities

The concerns and needs of victims are important for effective and successful community corrections. Community corrections must become active and progressive in developing and implementing policy that incorporates deliverable services to victims. This philosophy fosters the development of comprehensive services for both offenders and their victims, making the criminal justice system more responsive and humanistic to all.

Comprehensive strategies should employ all or part of victim services that start from the point of arrest to the point of releasing the offender from community supervision. These strategies include the following:

- addressing personal and professional barriers that inhibit effective victim services

- determining the phase in the criminal justice system during which probation and parole should provide services to victims

- assessing and developing interagency collaboration

- providing internal training

- providing interagency training and public awareness

- providing indirect and direct victim services

Barriers

Many professionals in the criminal justice system are unprepared to work with victims. They develop barriers that inhibit assistance and desensitize them to the plight of victims. Field officers may feel uncomfortable with the attendant emotional trauma of victimization and may feel unprepared to deal with it.

Many community corrections professionals receive little or no academic or vocational training in victim services. Most professional training in the criminal justice system focus on the offender. Trained community corrections officials are taught that services should be predominantly offender-based. Most colleges, universities, and community-based correctional agencies have little to offer students and practitioners in the area of victim service education and training. But, this is changing. In 1989, California State University at Fresno developed a certificate program in victimology. The University of South Carolina began offering such courses as part of their 1991 criminal justice curriculum. Community corrections agencies are starting to incorporate victim services as part of their initial and in-service training programs.

Community corrections should be aggressively and actively involved in the delivery of direct and indirect services to victims for many reasons, including the following (NOVA 1984):

1. Probation and parole departments interact with other criminal justice agencies, and probation staff have access to criminal justice information.

2. Probation and parole is a countywide or statewide community protection and casework agency.

3. Probation and parole is often linked to local services and resources throughout the community that could be helpful to victims.

4. Probation and parole departments have a history and proven track record with volunteerism.

5. Probation and parole officers are mandated by law to assist the court during the dispositional phase of a specific case. Victim information should be provided to the court at the time of sentencing.

6. Probation and parole departments have either legislatively or judicially mandated responsibilities in the area of financial restitution and are accountable for its collection.

7. Probation and parole departments understand the language of policies and procedures of other

Most victims, especially those of violent crimes, feel their lives and the lives of their families and friends have been irrevocably changed.

agencies within the criminal justice system with which victims and witnesses must deal.

8. Probation and parole departments should be involved in crime and delinquency prevention. Successful victim services can be an important element of prevention services.

Victims who take an active role can assist supervising officers in ensuring compliance with the supervision agreement. An aggressive restitution policy is a good illustration. Offenders learn accountability for their behavior by paying monetary restitution or symbolic restitution in the form of community service.

Community corrections administrators should realize that their constituents are not only the offenders, but the public as a whole. Both victims and offenders are members of the community. The public employs and empowers community corrections officials to deal with offenders for society's benefit. Community corrections cannot serve its intended goals without caring for victims who bear the consequences of crime.

Community corrections is the largest, fastest growing, most successful, and most popular correctional sanction (Cox 1985). The opportunity to serve a large portion of the overall victim population is within the capacity of community corrections officials.

The role of probation and parole services is perceived to be multiservice oriented. According to the National Organization for Victim Assistance (NOVA) (1984), "[t]he mission of probation and parole is to include delinquency and crime prevention, community education, dealing with the impact of crime, and building good community support for quality correctional services...the fundamental purpose of probation and parole services is to aid in reducing the incidence and impact of crime in the community." Providing services to victims could make the overall system of criminal justice more effective and efficient. "The fact remains that victim information and information regarding the impact of crime should be beneficial for the system and the victim" (NOVA 1984).

Effective community corrections must involve the public to the point where there is a "buy-in" and commitment on the part of private citizens in assisting the rehabilitation of the offender.

Community corrections should provide leadership in victim services. Probation and parole agencies are also in a natural position to collaborate and develop a relationship with victim services. There are obvious problems, such as role confusion, inadequate definition, overlapping of services, and competition between community corrections

and victim services for limited funding, that must be overcome (Shapiro, Alexander & Schuman 1988).

Probation and parole staff are uniquely trained as brokers for services, problem identifiers, and problem solvers. Because of their role in the criminal justice system, staff are experts in utilizing community resources to rehabilitate offenders. Staff members can achieve this goal regardless of the multiplicity of offender- or family-related problems.

An officer's main difficulty is lack of time and large offender caseloads (Cox 1985). Because of time constraints, many agencies have specialized their offender services (e.g., intensive supervision, domestic violence, sex offender, community service, electronic monitoring, high risk). As brokers for community services, they have developed expertise on community networking among various public and private helping agencies.

Many problems offenders experience (e.g., unemployment, substance abuse, financial difficulties, personal skills deficiencies, depression, and a conglomerate of other problems) are similarly experienced by victims of crime. Probation and parole officers should routinely help to link victims to these services by using existing resources. This would increase the effectiveness of probation and parole's response to the needs of the community.

When Victim Services Should Be Provided

Determining when an agency should or could provide services depends on many internal and external factors that govern agency policy and practice.

The commitment probation and parole administrators apply to victim services is strongly related to perceptions regarding the role probation and parole should serve. "If the administrator perceives the role or mission to be limited to recommending dispositions and to supervising offenders, then the concept of victim services is an alien one. However, if the mission is perceived to include delinquency and crime prevention, community education, dealing with the impact of crime and building good community support for quality correctional services, then the administrator will place a high priority on providing services to victims, particularly victims of violent crime" (NOVA 1984).

Agency administrative philosophy is based on many subjective and objective elements that change over time. The community corrections professional must develop a victim services package that has realistic implementation strategies. Progressive probation and parole practice recognizes that the purpose of community corrections does not adopt the narrow, traditional viewpoint, but adopts the view that probation and parole services should aid in reducing crime and the effect of crime on the community.

Most states have legislation mandating the types of services agencies are to provide, and who in the system of criminal justice is to provide them (NOVA 1988). Prevailing legislation is one of the best tools to decrease, if not eliminate, previously mentioned problems (e.g., role confusion, rivalry for funds, and jurisdictional restrictions) that develop between community corrections and other victim service providers.

Legislation should specify, from the point the crime is committed until the offender is released from the system, who is responsible for providing services and exactly what services a victim can expect from various providers. Typically, such legislation identifies providers and their responsibilities chronologically as the victim progresses through the criminal justice system. Probation and parole can potentially provide services from the point of the criminal incident, until the offender is released from correctional supervision.

Interagency Collaboration

Although community corrections may provide leadership in linking services to victims, it should be aware of assistance programs offered by established victim service groups so that efforts are not duplicated. The first task of any community corrections victim service provider should be to assess existing community resources that assist victims.

Interagency agreements should be put in writing, with responsibilities clearly assigned. Collaborative efforts serve to clarify roles, identify problems in service delivery (without placing blame), educate network members, and enhance information sharing.

The second task is to establish formalized communication networks and information sharing on a regular basis among community corrections and all victim service providers.

Third, probation and parole officials should seek, when possible, to augment or improve existing services.

Probation and parole professionals can provide services not only after the offender is sentenced to community supervision, but prior to sentencing when much of the trauma experienced by the victim takes place.

There are many reasons why collaborative networks should be formed among community corrections and victim service providers. "Role confusion, inadequate definition, and sometimes rivalry between community corrections and victim services for limited funding hamper effective service delivery to victims" (Shapiro, Alexander & Schuman 1988).

Working together, all victim service providers within the criminal justice system (law enforcement officers, prosecutors, judicial officials, corrections professionals) and outside the system (crisis intervention agencies, domestic violence shelters, psychological and financial services, personal advocacy assistance) must strive to provide the best services possible to victims.

There are basic principles and elements of collaboration that should be understood by all victim services providers within the realm of community corrections. Shapiro, Alexander, and Schuman (1988) have documented specific strategies to develop and assess collaboration community corrections and victim services agencies. There are four major principles of collaboration:

1. Collaboration is an ongoing process. It does not occupy a fixed place in time; it is continuously evolving. Continuous input, flexibility, and openness is required to adapt to and reflect local environmental and political shifts.

2. There are many approaches to collaboration. There are no right or wrong ways, just different ways. From locality to locality, or state to state, aspects of a collaborative effort vary. They reflect differences in the needs to be addressed and voids to be filled. The effort must address agency goals and resources, community resources and values, political context, and formality of the initial relationship.

3. Collaboration must respond to a need. Victim advocates and other key criminal justice and community officials (e.g., representatives from the judiciary and district attorney's offices, public defenders, and social service providers) must find a common denominator around which to rally. This may be an obvious void in service delivery or a perceived problem of communication. Whatever the need may be, it must be articulated. There should also be agreement about its significance, and the benefits to individual participants must be obvious. For example, the victim impact statement is of interest to the victim, probation and parole officers, the prosecutor, the judge, and the offender.

4. Collaboration requires initiative. A catalyst, usually in the form of a person acting on behalf of an agency, must initiate the collaborative process. The motivation to do so is often derived from a nagging need or crisis. Once the process is initiated, leadership must be sustained to ensure active participation. Such leadership can be visible or invisible, depending on the feasibility of adapting it to a given environment. An example of this is the involvement of Mothers Against Drunk Driving, which typifies the potential effect of a national catalyst.

As a complement to these four principles, the following elements are essential ingredients of victim service providers/community corrections collaboration:

1. Clarify role. The first step in a collaborative process is to delineate the formal and informal activities conducted by both community corrections and victim service providers. Underlying values of each agency must be articulated. Also, the current relationship among the various agencies must be established. It is helpful to explore perceptions and expectations among agencies.

2. Formalize interagency relationships. Once roles are clarified, it is important to clearly spell out which agency is responsible for what activities. Interagency agreements, referral forms, and other necessary documentation are needed to formalize responsibilities. A liaison from pertinent agencies (such as the victim service agency, the probation department, and the district attorney) should be designated to deal with day-to-day issues. This makes it easier to track information and solve problems immediately. It is useful to tap into an existing criminal justice group or, if necessary, to create a new one. This paves the way for unity and consolidated efforts in addressing crime victims' concerns.

3. Train staff. Training can be used to encourage sensitivity to victims' needs and to community corrections' mandates. For example, it would be useful for a probation officer to learn why it is so important to collect a victim impact statement. Conversely, learning about the constraints a probation and parole officer faces creates realistic expectations that a victim advocate can pass on to a victim.

4. Share information. After services have been integrated, staff have been trained, and specific programs designed to meet victim needs have been identified, the public should be told about these efforts. Public accessibility to this information encourages community response and provides an opportunity for citizens to take responsibility. Brochures, newspaper articles, and public speaking forums are natural mechanisms for ongoing communication. It is also a good practice to promote mutual awareness among other service providers, such as mental health counselors, who would benefit from referrals.

Internal Staff Training

As noted earlier, community corrections professionals receive little, if any, training in victim services even though they may work with victims daily. Within the past few years, several national victim advocacy organizations have developed training curricula for law enforcement officers, prosecutors, and other personnel and agencies in the criminal justice system who deal with victimization and staff services. The American Probation and Parole Association's "Offender Supervision and Victim Restitution Project" is an example of the type of comprehensive national victim services training curriculum needed for probation and parole.

Recent research identifies the training of probation and parole officers in victim-related services to be of paramount importance. In fact, a national survey (Shapiro, Omole & Schuman 1988) determined that 98 percent of community corrections agencies agreed that their officers should receive special training on how to deal with victims. The same researchers found the following broad recommendations in the area of officer training to be critically important:

1. Officers should become aware of the various legal alternatives that would result in more sensitivity to victims' needs.

2. Officers should be trained in learning alternative service options to meet victims' needs.

3. Officers should be trained in techniques that will help the offender feel responsibility for his or her crime against victims.

4. Officers should be trained to educate the criminal justice system and the public about victim service programs.

5. Officers should play a major role in educating judges about alternative victims' needs.

6. Officers should be trained on how to separate victims' needs from offender punishment.

Staff should understand that the long-term goal of community corrections is public service. Victims are an integral part of this service. Additionally, a training philosophy that must be instilled within every community corrections official is the concept of victims as their constituency.

Interagency Training and Public Awareness

Collaborative efforts provide training to all participants involved in various programmatic and agency objectives. Community corrections has a great desire and need to develop cooperative relationships with all victim service providers. The goal is to diminish role confusion and overlapping services. Thus, if the criminal justice system is to function as a system at all, the right hand needs to know what the left hand is doing.

Providing educational information and training to external victim service providers should be accomplished through many different types of forums, both formal and informal. External networking and training should be broad-based to reach all service providers.

A professional victim service provider training network should be established with the goal of educating each participating agency. Training participants should include those who are responsible for victim services:

- law enforcement

- prosecutors/court personnel

- community and institutional corrections

- private attorneys

- pastoral religious services

- domestic violence/rape/crisis intervention staff

- social assistance professionals

- medical and psychological professionals

Officers can use their expertise and experience to help victims who suddenly find themselves players in the criminal justice system. *(Officers on the left, victim on the right.)*

- volunteers

- substance abuse professionals

- personal advocacy groups for offenders and victims

- social/civic community organization members

- state and local service providers

Initially, training network participants should include formal presentations regarding agency services to victims. The network should hold monthly meetings and have one presentation per meeting. The format should encourage participants to ask questions and examine the program being presented. The presentations should illustrate positive changes or recommendations an agency may implement to improve services.

As the training network progresses, smaller committees should be formed that explore various avenues or issues related to common goals of the group as a whole. The use of the task force forum is one of the best tools available to quickly disseminate information and get direct feedback from participating members.

Network members do not have to limit themselves to formal meetings. Networking should explore alternatives to formal meetings, such as telephone conference calls, luncheon meetings, and meeting and networking during shared social events. All of these forms of communication can be conducted in the evening or on the weekends.

For mutual training activities and workshops, a staff member designated as an agency victim service representative should volunteer to be a presenter as part of the agenda for another agency's training function, committee meeting, or annual conference. The presentation should broadly examine all agency functions and, specifically, victim service efforts.

One of the most effective ways to educate and inform is by combining training efforts among various victim service provider groups. Many of the training components in victim services have common goals; this provides an excellent opportunity for cross-training. All service providers are dependent on each other for information. Through cross-training, cooperative assistance can also be established.

A speakers' bureau is another strategy for interagency training. The speakers' bureau should comprise staff trained in educating victim service providers not employed by the agency. The concept of the speakers' bureau should be well-publicized and marketed comprehensively.

All agencies should develop a multitude of resources that educate and inform various service providers of agency efforts in community corrections, specifically information about victim services provided by the agency. The following are some suggestions:

1. Brochures—One of the most effective tools to get the word out is brochures that describe the overall probation and parole system in addition to brochures that describe services to victims. Brochures produced in-house can be cost-effective. Information that will need periodic updating should be kept on a separate page that can be easily replaced, as needed, and inserted in the brochure.

2. One-page Informational Releases—One-page informational releases that describe agency services require very few resources to produce. When produced properly, they are effective and can be read quickly. The information can be readily updated to reflect changes in services, phone numbers, statistics, and contact persons. The information should be kept simple, brief, uncluttered, and easy to read. Informational releases and brochures should be mailed out periodically to all victim service providers.

3. Posters and Display Materials—Properly designed posters are effective marketing tools and can be displayed at events (i.e., Crime Victims' Rights Week), conferences, meetings, and certain public locations where traffic and visibility are high. National victim service organizations (i.e., the National Victim Center and NOVA) have display-ready materials that are generic enough to fit any agency's needs and are available at no charge with membership.

Visually depicting the agency's services with pictures, statistics, graphs, flow charts, and text provides a powerful tool to convey the agency's message. Every opportunity should be explored to display materials during information exchange sessions.

4. Package Stuffers—Package stuffers, such as pencils, pens, buttons, pins, rulers, and bumper stickers, distributed at conferences and meetings can contribute to public awareness. These marketing tools are daily reminders of the agency's efforts on behalf of victims of crime.

5. Audio and Video Tapes—If properly prepared, audio and video tapes serve as effective training and educational tools.

6. Slide Presentations—Visually depicting agency services to victims using slides is another interesting and cost-effective way to promote the agency's efforts. Slides may be duplicated and distributed with a script so that anyone from an officer to an administrator can make the presentation. Graphs and charts are easily converted to slides and should be incorporated into the presentation for variety.

7. Logo and Slogan—A catchy phrase and a symbolic logo of the program or agency goes a long way in getting nonagency staff and the public to remember and associate the agency with victim services.

8. Public Service Announcements—Community corrections officials should approach various public and private media organizations and request that they volunteer their services. Many local media and advertising companies will occasionally donate television time and talent, bulletin board advertising space, or print media advertising space to promote victim services and educate the public.

9. Availability to the Media—If approached knowledgeably, interactions with the media can be informative and helpful. Press releases should be distributed when visiting local newspaper, radio, and television stations.

10. Availability to the Public—Social clubs, churches, corporations, and professional groups are always looking for good presenters who have interesting news to share. The agency's public relations materials should state that the agency is able and willing to provide speakers on relevant issues. The materials should also include a contact phone number (a toll-free number, if possible).

Indirect and Direct Victims Services

If there is an unfulfilled demand for services or a deficiency in existing services, community corrections should provide these services from the earliest point in the system. Services should continue until the offender is released from supervision.

Services to the public and potential victims can begin prior to a criminal incident through community education. The goals are to promote awareness and prevent crime. Services can also promote awareness of resources available to victims. The agency's public relations materials can describe the incidence of crime and the tactics that can be used to protect oneself from crime.

Probation and parole services supervise the majority of convicted offenders and are in the position to keep the public informed about offenders. The public, criminal justice professionals, and victim service providers should be given information about ways in which to make communities safer and sanctions that hold offenders accountable and responsible. They should be informed and involved in the community corrections effort to ensure support of the unified goal to rehabilitate offenders in the community setting.

Crime often elicits a crisis response from victims for which a need for intervention services exists. Victims experience many problems from the criminal incident. Frequently, symptoms classically described as those associated with post-traumatic stress syndrome are experienced and need to be addressed.

Victims experience a wide range of needs in the aftermath of a crime, both short- and long-term. Typical needs and problems victims experience include the following:

- emergency financial assistance

- property repair

- crime scene cleanup

- the need for locating interpreters

- employment intervention

- creditor intervention

- child care

- transportation services

- contacting relatives and friends

- mental and medical referrals

- assistance in filing protection orders

- employment

Probation and parole officers are trained to identify problems, gather information, and address specific needs of individuals. They are the components in the criminal justice system that can guide victims through the somewhat alien system of criminal justice (Shapiro, Alexander & Schuman 1988).

The victim's first contact with the criminal justice system usually begins with the police. The police have traditionally served victims by providing information, referral, and property return (Waller 1990). When collaborative measures are established between the police and community corrections, referrals can be made by the police to probation and parole. Community corrections officers can use their training to identify problems, gather information, and help victims cope with the trauma, either in-house or by brokering for services.

Some things that can be done include the following:

1. Establish toll-free telephone hot lines. There should be one number where police, service providers, and victims can contact someone for assistance.

2. Use volunteers, combined with paid staff, to manage a team that can respond twenty-four hours a day.

3. Develop a community resource referral manual that comprehensively describes resources available for victims of crime. Needs assessment by community corrections officials should identify the various problems victims may experience and where direct and indirect services are to be provided.

Conclusion

Community corrections can provide many services to victims if progressive and enlightened changes in the criminal justice system continue to occur.

Many of the services to victims can be created and implemented with the existing talent and resources of probation and parole professionals. Providing services to crime victims is a challenge. Community corrections officials in the 1990s must be committed to the challenge and the long-range goals that will make the system more just, responsive, rehabilitative, and humanistic to both victims and offenders.

References

Cox, V. 1985. *Introduction to corrections*, 3d edition. Englewood Cliffs, N.J.: Prentice-Hall.

National Organization for Victim Assistance. 1984. *Role of Probation in Victim Services*. Policy paper. Washington, D.C.: NOVA.

————. 1988. *Victim legislative summary*. Survey report. Washington, D.C.: NOVA.

Shapiro, C., D. Alexander, and A. M. Schuman. 1988. *Making it work: Addressing victim concerns through community corrections programs*. Unpublished research paper.

Shapiro, C., O. Omole, and A. M. Schuman. 1988. *The role of victim and probation: Building a collaborative relationship, a summary of survey results*. Unpublished research paper.

Waller, E. 1990. The police: First in aid? In *Victims of crime: Problems, policies, and programs*, ed. A. J. Lurigio, W. G. Skogan, and R. C. Davis. Newbury Park, Calif.: Sage Publications.

12

Managing Change in Probation and Parole

By Donald G. Evans

Probation and parole, the mainstays in community corrections, are undergoing major changes in their approaches to offender management and services to the community. The past two decades have seen the field adapt to shifts in philosophy and sentencing practices and learn to accommodate new fiscal realities. This adaptation has occurred in a context of fiscal constraint, rethinking of the objectives of probation and parole, and public demand for increased accountability.

These components and their affect on the future of probation and parole services will be examined in this chapter. In doing so the current correctional crisis and the renewed emphasis on community corrections as a policy and program alternative to this crisis will be visited. The factors promoting change and factors assisting management of change in probation and parole services will also be discussed. The chapter will conclude with a look at the role of the community in the future development of probation and parole.

In Chapter 1, "History of Probation and Parole," Cohn indicated that the development of probation and parole was a response to the perceived failure or inadequacies of early correctional practice, specifically the failure of incarceration. Corrections is again faced with a crisis—the unprecedented growth in offender populations. Correctional facilities in most jurisdictions are crowded. Many

departments of corrections face court orders limiting capacity and operate under legislated population caps.

The issue of prison crowding will likely dominate the correctional landscape for the rest of the decade. As Martin and Goldstein point out in their chapter, "Intermediate Sanctions and Probation," the prison population is now over three times that recorded in the seventies. There are over a million offenders incarcerated in U.S. facilities with no relief in sight.

A number of events have contributed to this rapid increase in prison populations.

1. Sentencing guidelines have had the effect of lengthening and making determinate many criminal sentences. A number of states as well as the federal government have enacted stricter guidelines with the result of incarcerating more offenders.

2. Drug enforcement through tougher legislation and prosecution has resulted in drug offenders representing nearly half the prison populations.

3. Public attitudes and government response have shifted from a rehabilitative approach to a more punitive one.

Most correctional policymakers agree that imprisonment is not necessarily the most effective sanction. Many believe incarceration should be reserved for offenders who have committed serious offenses and who present a risk to the public. In the 1980s, efforts were made to use

Donald G. Evans, *past president of the American Probation and Parole Association, is assistant deputy minister of the Ministry of the Solicitor General in Ontario, Canada.*

probation as an alternative to incarceration. Creative use of the conditional aspects of probation allowed judges and probation officers to develop innovative approaches to offender management. A number of program initiatives were launched. The main programs in that period were community service orders and restitution. By the end of the 1980s the increase in probation caseloads was dramatic, with no corresponding increase in fiscal resources. The prison crowding crisis had now been reproduced in probation.

Martin and Goldstein outline the latest developments in efforts to ease crowding pressures in the prison and probation setting. Efforts are underway to develop a range of sanctions that lie between probation and prison.

It is unclear at this time whether efforts to develop intermediate sanctions and to enhance probation and parole supervision with new techniques will alleviate crowding in prisons or exacerbate the problem. Improved means for detection of violators and a zero tolerance for drug use may not relieve population pressures because incarceration is the alternative to probation or parole. Many violators are returned to prison. These new approaches need to be evaluated. An important development in probation and parole is commitment to research and to the development of standards. The American Correctional Association, the National Institute of Corrections, and the American Probation and Parole Association are leaders in this regard.

Persistent crowding of jails and prisons has forced corrections to change its approach to offender management. Three other major factors have also contributed to the need for change.

The first of these factors is scarce financial resources for community corrections programs. The scarce correctional dollar makes it necessary to learn to do things differently, to manage more with less, and in some instances to simply do less. Learning to manage in this environment is a major challenge, and future community correctional managers will have to adapt to this new reality.

Demographic changes are also affecting the way corrections delivers probation and parole services. Increased minority populations demand a more culturally diverse and sensitive workforce. The ability to deal with offenders in their own language is becoming more important. Agency hiring practices and training programs are changing to meet these new demands. The characteristics of today's offenders present challenges as well: there are more violent offenders being supervised in the community, offenders who have a range of personal and social problems. Programs for substance abusers, offenders who are themselves victims of abuse, and offenders suffering from

AIDS are needed today and represent areas of specialization that call on probation and parole to work closely with other social services agencies.

The final factor that provides an impetus for change is the increased interest in accountability. The public is demanding that all its institutions be held accountable, and communities want assurances that their tax dollars are being used wisely and effectively. The focus on public safety has highlighted probation and parole and how offenders are supervised in the community. Improvements in offender classification and assessment systems have greatly enhanced corrections' ability to be accountable and to provide levels of supervision that enhance public safety. The renewed interest in service for victims has also made probation and parole more cognizant of its need to respond to the interests of the community. (See Chapter 11, "Victims.")

These factors have demanded changes in the way corrections professionals conduct their work, manage the workplace, and develop staff. Fortunately, there are also factors assisting efforts to manage these changes.

First, new management approaches that are emerging from the "total quality management" movement are offering probation professionals a method for managing change. The major elements for managing organizational change are universal; it is the commitment and the application of the techniques that are crucial. The universal factors are as follows:

- streamlining programs—removing unnecessary and ineffective programs

- defining mission and values—creating and nurturing a vision of the organization that communicates clearly what the agency is doing

- implementing continuous improvement programs —striving for excellence means investing in programs that will improve services and upgrade quality of staff

- focusing on client service—keeping in mind why the organization exists and who the client is makes it clear that probation and parole agencies serve more than one type of client and therefore need to offer a range of services to the offender, courts, and public

- reengineering the workplace—using information technology to develop more effective processes in the workplace (e.g., using laptop computers instead of probation notebooks) involving staff—soliciting the opinions and ideas of all staff is critical to developing better ways to deliver services (this also involves fostering teamwork among staff and providing them training)

Managing change requires that once the need for change is recognized, a consensus for change is built. This includes the development of effective communication strategies and clearly defined consultation objectives that reach out to staff and stakeholders.

Staff and supervisors should be aware of the key elements in how to master change. They include the following:

1. Recognize that change is occurring.

2. Identify the changes that affect delivery of service, the profession, and personal plans.

3. Determine the form of the change (e.g., structural or cyclical). Structural change is demanding; it is usually accompanied by a major change in the way things function.

4. Adopt changes according to the importance of their effect and probability of occurrence.

5. View changes as opportunities to respond to new demands and expectations.

Organizations that successfully manage change operate on the basis of clearly defined objectives and an explicit statement of values. They are able to handle conflict in the normal course of events. Management and staff in such organizations have a high tolerance for ambiguity and complexity. Administrators in these organizations are concerned for staff and recognize that management has to meet organizational objectives as well as human needs.

The Future of Probation and Parole

The future of probation and parole depends on how successfully change is managed in the work environment. Enlisting the support and help of others can significantly affect response to change. This means agencies need to define their communities and ask their help in dealing with the issues and demands facing an overburdened correctional system. Communities need to be informed of the benefits of probation and parole and enlisted to support community corrections initiatives.

The support of a number of key groups is important in handling change in probation and parole:

1. Legislators can assist by supporting and sponsoring legislative initiatives similar to the Community Corrections Acts that some jurisdictions have adopted. Agencies need to supply legislators information and facts that will enable them to respond to critics.

2. Members of the judiciary make strong allies because they are responsible for determining appropriate sentences. They should be consulted for their feedback regarding appropriate alternatives to incarceration.

3. Making contacts in local neighborhoods through the leadership in local government, business, service clubs, churches, and neighborhood associations can be very productive. Reaching out to the community helps put the "community" in community corrections.

4. It is important to research and establish contacts with human service agencies. These agencies are valuable in the delivery of services to offenders under supervision. (See Chapter 10, "Probation and Parole and the Community.")

Field officers should be involved in public education efforts to develop a constituency of support for the work of probation and parole. An involved community helps corrections meet the demands of resource constraints through volunteers and support for programs.

Accountability is achieved by informing and involving the community. Probation and parole functions now take victims and victims groups into account. Many are also looking for ways to get the community involved in crime prevention. Some jurisdictions are adopting the approach of community policing. Partnerships with community groups and other local services work to identify, solve, and assess community needs and are proving to be an effective way to make communities safer.

A community approach to probation and parole can address the fear citizens have of being victimized by explaining what probation and parole professionals do, how offenders are supervised, and how community members get answers to their questions about offenders supervised in their community.

The future of probation and parole is promising. Today's probation and parole agencies have proven their adaptability and willingness to change.